MEEKS

a novel

GABRIEL TAIT

DEDICATION

For my family

Shannon, Preston, Lucas, Evan and Mackenzie

And for my brother

PROLOGUE

A solitary horse stood watch, blinking at the darkness. The horse's muscles ached from the afternoon's work, and although he had learned not to perceive the men as threatening over time, something within him resisted their attempts to mount him. This aspect of his nature, combined with his feral strength and arresting appearance had solidified his worth. He was a dangerous horse. Day had long since turned to night. All was calm. Dew droplets had slicked the grass, forming a fresh glaze, a favourite for grazing. As he lowered his heavy head for a nibble, the scent reached his nostrils.

The cowboy awakens to tend his flock.

Despite an unconscious effort to roll away from the pain, the cowboy jolted himself awake with a scream. His arm. If he hadn't been sure it was broke, he was damn sure now. Fortunately, the pill bottle lay within reach, the trailer was small and his bed smaller. With two pills down his gullet, he lay his head back on the pillow and inhaled. He stayed still waiting for the pills to slow his breathing before he started poking around his arm like he does when under the hood at the side of the road. He has done this many times, on both car and machine. His father had taught him. Nothing seemed out of place, but the swelling was bad.

He had taken quite a fall, yet his arm showed no bend in a direction that it shouldn't. He would seek out the local prairie skinner in the morning to get it tended to, but for now, the pills would have to do. His head worried him more than his arm. He recalled stepping up to the trailer after the accident, and how he had braced himself against the spinning and the nausea. He didn't remember falling asleep. Not a good sign. He wondered if his arm might have saved his life as he hoisted himself up to a sitting position on the sagging mattress, like Buddha. Had he not rolled his full weight over it, he might never have woken up. Head injuries can take you in your sleep. His father told him that. What he really needed was to be awakened every few hours, but he had no one.

In time with his breathing, he mentally went through his checklist: *My name is Cooper. The date is June 24th, 1979. I am in the township of Kinglin. I ride horses for the rodeo.* Other things were missing. Small things. Portable memories he had collected over time and had carried with him.

The wet bandage surprised him. He unraveled the headpiece and located the wound. The bleeding had stopped, which relieved him some. The pills dulled the throbbing behind his eye sockets, working their way to his arm. Cooper reached for the nightstand light, accidentally knocking over a forgotten bottle, causing the remaining beer to spill into his upright boot. *I need to consider another line of work*, he thought.

Cooper kept the lights off because the dark helped. In the trailer's blackness, he mistook the blood-soaked sheets for sweat. He could hear the horses agitating in their pen. He liked having his trailer close to them. Since childhood, he found their conversations comforting and knew well enough when something was wrong.

Must be those boys from earlier. If his old man had locked horns with a crew like that in his day, he would sure as shit have taken the whip to them and learned them a thing or two.

Cooper had an intimate knowledge of his father's whip. But only when the occasion called for it, you understand.

Cooper rose to his stockinged feet and took three shaky steps toward the trailer door but abruptly halted to puke up into the sink. When he finished, he coaxed cool water from the tap, swished, spat it out, and washed the dried blood from his eyes.

He swung open the trailer door, feeling the prairie air cool his skin, where the water had washed helping with the *throb throb throb*. No signs of trouble were immediately visible, but the horses were worked up, trotting within the confines of the fence.

"Whoa! Easy! Easy!" Cooper shouted as he approached the gate, trying to calm them, unable to raise his broken arm. He turned the peg to open the gate and then smelled it. Fire. The cowboy no longer felt the pain in his skull.

PART ONE

PRAIRIE 1979

CHAPTER 1

"Without any street signs visible, there was little chance the fire department could have arrived in time to save the victim."

- Fairlawn City Intelligencer, June 26, 1979

SATURDAY, JUNE 23, 1979, 9:30 AM

Ranleigh Echo Meeks opened his eyes, breakfast was well underway. Grandma wanted him to be well-fed and cleaned up for the long day ahead. Ranleigh loved waking up to the smell of her cooking. Unlike at home, where meals were usually haphazard, she always prepared a generous spread and more than he could finish. Home, which now seemed like a distant dream, never made him feel as hungry as the prairie did. Despite the fact that at home he often left for school without eating, and if a proper meal was ever served, it would only be on Sundays—usually consisting of KFC, potato salad, and a bag of chips. Those meals felt like holiday meals because they happened so rarely. After eating, he would succumb to a sleepy feeling, much like after Christmas dinner. Ranleigh didn't like that feeling. Feeling full made him too relaxed and therefore vulnerable to attack. At home, he preferred being hungry. At home, he preferred to be *awake*.

Ranleigh checked his digital watch, the one adorned with two robots from the space movie. The time was 9:32 AM, displayed in a fading red glow. The battery would never get changed. His grandmother must have been hollering for a while, but he hadn't heard.

"Are you up?"

"Yes, Grandma, I'm up," Ranleigh replied. He could hear the concerned swish of her slippers, like a brush moving across a snare drum, as she padded her way down the hall toward the enclosed front porch where he slept during his visits.

"Come and join me for breakfast, will you? We have quite a day ahead of us."

"Okay, Grandma. I'll be there in a minute." His grandmother poked her head in, gave him a quizzical once over, decided he was awake, and headed back towards the kitchen, quickening the tempo. As Ranleigh squinted towards the porch windows, waiting for his eyes to adjust, he pondered the vast yet immediate prairie sky. It was nothing like home, he thought—it felt like living in a gigantic snow globe.

"It's not for everyone," she had once told him. A car rolled by, crunching gravel and stirring up the dust in its wake. The passing car and the neighbour's barking dog were doing their best to disrupt the silence, *but breaking up the silence here would be like trying to break up the sky*, Ranleigh thought.

The kitchen was tucked away at the back of the house, added as an extension in the nineteen-fifties. The room was reliably cold, even in the summer. His grandfather had purportedly built it himself, out of spite. It didn't match the rest of the house in any way, except for the fact that it was attached to it. The design was what would later be called a mid-century modern attempt, with checkerboard floor tiles, and a wall-hung refrigerator that had ceased to function years ago and now served as an elongated cupboard above the sink. Two additional gleaming steel cupboards stood like sentries on either side. The roof was sloped.

Since inheriting the house from her father, who died

tragically of a heart attack while knee-deep in snow chopping wood, his grandma had always lived there. Her father had built the home after unintentionally becoming one of the founding residents of the town of Kinglin at the turn of the century, making her family somewhat of a big deal - a fact that his grandpa resented fiercely.

Grandma possessed two distinguishing features that set her apart from most women. She stood half a foot taller than the average woman of her era and had a full head of snow-white hair that had turned before she reached the age of thirty. She never dyed it and wore it proudly. Grandma was educated, direct, fearless, and kind-hearted. She didn't tolerate fools and insisted on things being done the right way. Ranleigh believed that if she had been born in his time, she could have achieved more and seen more if not for the limitations imposed on women in her day.

Ranleigh seemed to understand by the way she said the word, that *limitations* had meant *men*. Despite those limitations, she had done quite well for herself and would have been considered a women's libber in modern terms. If Ranleigh were ever to have a daughter, she would owe this woman a debt.

"Ranleigh, what's the matter? You've barely touched anything. Are you feeling unwell?"

"No, Grandma. Just tired, I guess."

"I've told you not to stay up watching television. I have never understood the fascination. Sitting in front of that thing with your mouth hanging open when there is a whole world out there to see. Maybe I should get rid of it if you're that tired. You're the only one who watches it anyway."

"No, Grandma, please don't. I'm fine. Probably wasn't even the TV. Maybe it was the..." Ranleigh blanched. He seemed to have locked up inside. His grandmother looked up from the pulling of a loose thread from her housecoat, shocked to see a boy's face curdle that way.

"It was what, Ranleigh?" Nothing. She instinctively snapped her bony fingers at him, her rings dangling below her knuckles and bracelets jingling. "Ranleigh!" Snap. "Ranleigh!" snap jingle snap.

Ranleigh was silent but eventually turned his head, recognizing her presence. He was coming back to himself, and a warm sense of relief washed over her, unclenching her heart.

"Ranleigh, what's the matter, dear?" she asked, clapping her hands. "Ranleigh?"

"What did you say?" He felt as though he had lost a bit of time somewhere.

When he later reflected on the experience, it reminded him of playing the card game War. Every card was always accounted for—his pile, his friend's pile, and the cards they battled over in the middle. When he was losing, he had only lost a portion of his cards, figuring he would get them back later in the game. This felt something like that, though not exactly the same. Not quite playing with a full deck, in other words.

"You scared me, Ranleigh. Gave me quite a fright. We were talking about the television, do you remember?" Her last sentence sounded more panicked than she would ever admit. "Let me feel your forehead."

She sprang out of her chair with the agility and speed of a woman half her age. Standing in front of him, she rested the backs of her fingers on Ranleigh's forehead. Her hand felt cool and comforting but somewhat distant. He would have preferred her palm. And because he felt her distance, Ranleigh resisted the urge to wrap his arms around her waist and hug her.

"Maybe we should skip going to the rodeo today. I could set you up in the living room on the couch with a TV tray, and you could just rest. What do you think?" She wasn't so much asking him as holding the question outside of herself, examining it from different angles.

"Aww, Grandma, I was really looking forward to it. I feel okay, and I'll just be walking around and looking at stuff. I'm just tired."

She peered at him over her glasses, while returning to her

chair. "I'm not so sure. I made plans to meet Verna there, but I don't want to leave you alone if you're ill."

This was a good sign. Ranleigh knew that with older people, duty always prevailed. The only way she wouldn't pick up her friend Verna and drive her to the rodeo was if he was puking his guts out and running a fever of, like, a hundred and twenty. He could almost see her turning this over in her mind, absentmindedly wringing her hands in her lap. Definitely a good sign. There would be few things worse than being stuck indoors watching summer daytime television while hearing the screams pour out from the midway rides across the highway. Rubbing her hands together meant that she hadn't made a final decision yet. If there was ever a moment to tip the scales in his favour, it was now.

"We wouldn't want to ruin Verna's day just because I'm tired," he said, trying a different approach. Her narrowing gaze indicated her suspicion. Her hands grew still in her lap. Not good. She knew what he was trying to do. Quickly switching strategies, Ranleigh opted for honesty. Truth seemed to work best with her, unlike at home where it rarely had any effect. There wasn't much truth at home.

"Sorry, Grandma. Look, I really am feeling much better. I was up for a bit in the middle of the night because I had a bad dream. It was really weird, I was in some kind of dark hospital walking around the hallways, but it didn't last long, and I went right back to sleep. Maybe you're right and I'm coming down with a cold or something. But the rodeo is practically across the street, and if I get any worse, I'll come straight home. That way, we won't disappoint Verna, and I can still see some of it. I love staying here with you, and I like it when we play cards and all the things you bake for me, but there isn't much to do here. I was really looking forward to it. So, can we?"

She softened a little, maybe just enough, and the worry lines on her forehead retreated to their usual hiding place.

"Yes, all right, Ranleigh," she relented. "You can go with Verna and me today. But one's health is the most important thing. Take that to heart. Nothing is more important. So, if I see even the slightest sign that you're taking a turn for the worse, we will come straight home without any arguments from you. Do we have an agreement?"

"Yes," Ranleigh smiled.

"Promise?"

"Yes, I promise."

Throughout their time together, she had emphasized the significance of a promise with the fervour of a born-again street preacher, like the ones he had seen with their bullhorns and sandwich boards next to the new Eaton Centre on Yonge Street. And promise rule number one: You never break a promise to a child. Ranleigh tried to think of a time when she had broken a promise to him, but with a feeling he would later come to know as respect, he could not think of one.

"Okay, then." She clapped her hands on her lap, straightened her back, swung her legs out from under the table, and stood. They were going.

CHAPTER 2

Ranleigh and his grandmother locked the back door and headed for her car. A few days prior, she had handed him a flyer inviting all the townsfolk to the Kinglin Rodeo. Inside the car, out of boredom, he looked over the flyer, which he had left on the seat of the car. The seats were hot and smelled of leather. Ranleigh rolled down his window.

The Kinglin Rodeo, celebrating its seventy-first year, had opened in 1908, making it only a few years older than Ranleigh's grandmother—an image he found difficult to picture. It was even harder to imagine her attending the rodeo at his age, possibly with her seldom-mentioned father.

According to the flyer, they had missed the free pancake breakfast sponsored by the Merchants of Kinglin, which had ended at nine. Ranleigh felt a pang of guilt for oversleeping and inconveniencing his grandmother by making her cook when they could have eaten at the rodeo. However, he didn't feel bad that Verna was going to miss breakfast mostly because Verna didn't seem to like anything anyway. And besides, he had never seen her eat anything more substantial than a tea biscuit. In fact, he couldn't be sure if he had ever seen her eat anything at all. Since the rodeo spanned two days, Ranleigh decided to set his watch alarm to ensure they wouldn't miss the pancakes tomorrow.

Glancing at the list, he noticed they had also missed the Horse Show and the Grand Slam Baseball Tournament, an event his grandmother had tried unsuccessfully to get him signed up for. Although the tournament was open to all ages, Ranleigh didn't feel like joining. Ranleigh never played any sports at home and felt nervous about playing with a bunch of people he didn't know. He especially didn't like the idea of walking up to the plate, bat in hand with all eyes on him. The next item on the list was the Cattle Show, and they might still make that if they hurried. The midway would open at eleven, but Ranleigh knew not to hold his breath where Verna Hewitt was concerned, they still had to pick her up and she was never ready on time.

Verna Hewitt resided in a house similar to his grandma's. Both houses held minor historical significance in the town, as Verna's father and Ranleigh's great-grandfather had built their respective homes in the same year and were among the first families to settle in the area. Although Grandma and Verna had grown up together, they were never friends. Only in recent years had they started spending time together, and lately, they had become somewhat inseparable, which Ranleigh found odd. Despite being younger, Verna was nothing like his grandmother. She was what people called old-fashioned. Ranleigh figured that, like most people her age, she just wasn't any good with change. He imagined her as old-fashioned even when she was a young girl.

Verna Hewitt was a pretentious woman who took immense pride in her family's role in practically founding the town (as she would put it). The way she talked about her family she almost had you believing that they had a hand in founding not only the town, but the country itself. And because of this, she never let an opportunity pass to remind the current residents of Kinglin about her family's place at the top of the pecking order.

During her weekly visits to GREEN'S grocery store, Verna practically expected the red carpet to be rolled out for her. Upon entering, she would tap her cane three times on the brown linoleum floor, summoning the manager. Annoyed and slightly cowed, the poor man would reluctantly walk her down aisle by torturous aisle, pushing the cart and hanging on each of her specific instructions.

Verna would demand the manager check expiration dates on milk, cheese, and eggs, and she insisted that he handpick the finest fruits and vegetables for her, which were never good enough and always too expensive. Once satisfied with her selections, she would have the manager cut the line and carefully load her items onto the belt, rolling them to his most seasoned cashier. Of course, the store manager never permitted the elderly and somewhat confused-looking volunteer from the old age home to pack Verna's bags but would always handle it himself.

Finally, the manager would escort her directly to her car, gingerly placing each parcel in the trunk, the bags resembling a line of newborn babies in a maternity ward. He would have breathed a deep sigh of relief upon her departure if she hadn't been in the habit of peeling out of the parking lot leaving him to choke and sputter on exhaust fumes without so much as a thank you. And never any tip.

On Sunday mornings, Verna Hewitt could always be found at *her* church. Although she was never on time, the minister wouldn't dare begin his sermon until she settled into her seat at the front, left-hand aisle pew. The minister feared only two things in this world: Almighty God and Verna Hewitt. Once she was comfortably situated, certain that everyone had soaked up her entrance, she would grin and tap her cane three times on the grey, stone floor, giving a slight nod to indicate she was ready for the sermon to commence.

As Ranleigh's grandmother parked the car in front of the Hewitt house, he checked his watch again. The red digits were fading and hard to see in the daylight. 10:18 AM. While the rodeo was only a four-minute drive from their location, Ranleigh was beginning to doubt they would make it in time for the grand opening of the midway.

Aware that Verna Hewitt would be in less of a hurry than usual due to the rodeo committee's recent vote to do away with the official ribbon-cutting ceremony—a change that had horrified Verna—Ranleigh knew she otherwise would have been waiting on her porch at six in the morning and he might have stood a chance of arriving at the Midway on time. In rodeo's past Verna had always stood high on the wooden platform, surveying the perpetually insufficiently sized crowd, oversized gold-plated scissors in hand, ready to entertain them with stories of their founding father—her father. After a long speech and with great flair, she would sever the oversized ribbon to a light smattering of applause and crying babies, marking the start of yet another Kinglin Rodeo.

The Hewitt house was much larger than his grandmother's. This had been the source of ongoing contention between their fathers when the girls were in prairie school. Harold Hewitt had tricked Ranleigh's great-grandfather into believing their houses would be the same size by showing him a phony set of architectural plans. It became apparent only after the frames were erected that Harold intended to build the larger house.

Ranleigh couldn't decide whether the foreboding appearance of the Hewitt house stemmed from its design or the current occupant who resided within. Sitting in the car, gazing up at the ancient, freshly painted wraparound porch, Ranleigh concluded it was likely both. Verna Hewitt and the house were inseparable. You could no more separate them than you could salt from the ocean. Ranleigh often wondered what would happen to the house when Ms. Hewitt finally joined her forebears on that great rolled-out red carpet in the sky. He imagined it falling into a terrible state of disrepair, a haunted house that children would dare each other to approach on Halloween night.

"Ranleigh," his grandmother's voice interrupted his thoughts. "Why don't you go and see if Ms. Hewitt is ready?

And Ranleigh, give her a hand getting to the car."

"Do I have to?" Ranleigh groaned.

"Yes, Ranleigh. You're a young gentleman, after all. And as you well know, Ms. Hewitt isn't as spry as she used to be and might need your help," she replied.

Ranleigh scrutinized the house, grasped the car door handle, then started making his way up the stone path. As he mounted the first creaky step, it occurred to him that he had never been inside the Hewitt house and very much wished to keep it that way. Ranleigh offered a silent prayer that she would be waiting at the door, cane in hand and ready to go. Before he had the chance to lift the gigantic brass knocker, a voice barked from somewhere inside.

"Who's there?"

Ranleigh could never understand why some old people felt the need to put kids through their paces. It was obvious that she knew they were coming to pick her up and that his grandmother was never one to be late. It wasn't as though Verna Hewitt had overslept and was rushing around at the last minute to get ready and had lost track of time. She had likely been awake before the roosters if she had even slept at all. And somehow, *he knew that*. He knew she had been up at four, saying her prayers. He also knew that for the past hour or so, she had absolutely nothing to do and was silently waiting in that cheerless, dank living room for his knock.

"It's Ranleigh, Ms. Hewitt," he called back in the sweetest voice he could muster, hoping that an attempt at extreme politeness might get her moving.

"RANLEIGH WHO?"

"It's Ranleigh Meeks, Ms. Hewitt. Grandma and me are picking you up," the sweetness already beginning to sour.

"GRANDMA AND 'I'," she bellowed.

"Yes. Okay. Right. Grandma and I are here to take..."

"Just one minute, young man," she interrupted. "I'll be right with you!" Ranleigh heard the latch slide on the other side of the door. He took a breath as he watched it swing open, like a big yawning mouth, ready to swallow him. And there stood

17

Verna Hewitt, looming like a tongue in the dark cavern.

She stood at about five feet four inches tall, a round woman with a large bosom that appeared as one breast, not two. She had thickset legs and very large hands. She looked like an umpire, scrutinizing your every move and ready to call you out at the drop of a hat. Her baseball mitt-sized hand held a cane, and her eyes were dark and hollow. She wore round, gold-rimmed glasses that were too large for her face, even by '70s standards. Her lips formed a permanent scowl, and the pearl necklace she wore seemed to glow and float in the darkness of the foyer.

"Come in, Ranleigh, my boy. Won't you?" she didn't wait for a reply. "I'm just about ready. I'll just fetch my purse and turn out the lights. Have a seat there," she pointed to the living room with her cane. "I won't be a minute."

The living room was darker than the foyer, and Ranleigh couldn't figure out which lights she needed to turn off. That was another thing he had noticed about old people—they were always turning out the lights. In addition to barely being able to see anything, the air was thick with dust, coating his tongue and spreading down his throat like strep. As his eyes adjusted, he managed to feel his way into the living room and find a seat on one of the large couches. Ranleigh felt small in this room. While his grandmother's house was large but cozy, this place was cavernous and unwelcoming.

Verna Hewitt made her way back through the dining room, crossed a large carpet displaying a striking Canadian Native motif, and settled into a large chair directly across from Ranleigh.

"Good morning, Ranleigh. It's good to see you, young man. Your grandmother will be pleased that you are back here this summer. Are you looking forward to the rodeo today?" she inquired.

"Yes, Ms. Hewitt, I sure am. I can't wait to get there!" Ranleigh led.

"That's good. That's very good, boy," Verna nodded absentmindedly as she looked around the room, shifting her gaze from object to object.

Her eyes settled on a lampshade with an ivory skirt dangle, then travelled to the ornately carved stone fireplace. There was no rhyme or reason to her gaze. She looked at every object as if she had never seen them before. She seemed to be looking everywhere except at Ranleigh, and she didn't appear to be in any hurry to leave. This was going to be a slow process. It was already a slow process.

CHAPTER 3

SATURDAY, JUNE 23, 1979, 10:48 AM

His heart racing, he bolted out of the house, taking the porch steps two at a time. It hadn't taken long for Ranleigh to realize that Verna wasn't admiring the works of art or the furniture in the room. The room was too dark to see much anyway. Too dim to see practically anything, but she was looking hard. The musty odour inside reminded him of the garage back home, and it made him feel queasy. He hated that garage.

Verna continued her examination of the room like she had never seen it before, then suddenly became aware that she was not alone. Fixing her stare on him, she demanded to know what game he thought he was playing. Ranleigh sat paralyzed, unable to come up with an answer that could get them out of the house and to his grandmother's car. After a moment of stillness, Verna burst into a giggle, like a little girl.

Questions flooded Ranleigh's young mind. Where was his grandma? Why hadn't she come to check on him? Why hadn't she at least honked the horn? The answer was simple, honking the horn would be impolite. More silence. Ranleigh found himself praying for an escape from the Hewitt house while

Verna scrutinized him closely, struggling to stifle her laughter.

"Yes, Ranleigh. I suppose you're right. We wouldn't want to be late now, would we?" Ranleigh hadn't uttered a word. And then, the giggles returned. "I know you're not from here," Verna said, once her laughter was under control.

"Yes, ma'am. That's right. I'm not from around here. I'm from Toronto. I only come here once a year," Ranleigh answered.

"That's not what I mean, boy!" she shouted, startling Ranleigh. He had been tracing the Native motif on the carpet with the heel of his Kodiak, in an attempt to avoid her stare. "That's not what I mean at all."

Ranleigh fought an urge to run.

"I don't know what game you're playing and I'm not sure exactly where it is we are, but I should be at the hospital." No argument there. "I have patients to attend to. They DEPEND on me and if I'm not there, some of them could DIE! Can you understand that, boy? You of all people should be able to understand that. What time is it?"

Ranleigh looked at the digits on his watch glowing brightly in the dark living room and answered, "10:39."

"In the morning or at night?"

"It's morning, Ms. Hewitt."

"Well, that's a relief. Looks like I'm not missing my shift after all. I'm the overnight nurse. The day nurse is Charlene, and Charlene knows her stuff, boy. But if I'm not working I should be sleeping, and not sitting here with you. And so should you. And you should probably know, you are so ill. You are a very, very sick boy." She giggled again.

CHAPTER 4

SATURDAY, JUNE 23, 1979, 10:58 AM

Piling Verna into the car took some time for Ranleigh and his grandmother. As they pulled into the rodeo grounds, they struggled to find a parking spot near the entrance, which forced them to walk. In 1979, accessible parking was a long way off.

Once they entered through the gates, Ranleigh's grandmother gave him a pleasant surprise. She handed him a five-dollar bill, an amount much more than he had expected. The rides would open soon, and he hoped to buy enough tickets to try most of them. If he had any change left, he might even get a doughnut from the nearby bake sale tent. He thanked his grandma and nodded at Verna before turning to make a clean getaway.

"Ranleigh," his grandmother called after him. He stopped in his tracks and turned to face her. "Yes, Grandma?"

"Ms. Hewitt and I will be in the Grand Pavilion until lunchtime. I think they'll have most of the tables set up by now, and Ms. Hewitt would like to say hello to the organizers." *I bet she would*, Ranleigh thought to himself. "That is where we will be if you need us. If not, we'll see you for lunch, a cold plate at one o'clock. Have fun, Ranleigh, but stay out of trouble. And if you feel sick again, come and find me and we are heading straight back home."

"Don't worry, Grandma, I'm fine" Ranleigh replied. And I'd watch yourself too, Grandma. No telling what Verna Hewitt might do now that she thinks that you, me, the cows, the horses, and the cold plate lunch aren't real at all and that she needs to work the night shift at some hospital.

Freedom. Ranleigh breathed in deeply. The unfamiliar scent of hay and manure, a smell he wasn't used to coming from the city, made him feel slightly queasy, but with all the people donning their cowboy hats and boots, he decided to get into the spirit of things.

Making his way toward the ticket booth, he saw the rides were starting up, relieved that he had made it in time. This was what he had come for, and if he saw a bucking bronco or two, that would be all right. As long as the cowboy put on a good show and was thrown sky high, Evel Knievel style, it would be something to see.

Approaching the ticket booth, loud music blared through the sound system, but not the country music he had expected. *Tragedy, when you pick your nose and your head explodes, it's tragedy.* He knew that one from the radio and the schoolyard. The movie Grease had come out the previous summer, but he was too young to get into Saturday Night Fever. A friend's older brother told him the movie was restricted because some guy commits suicide.

The ticket booth was designed to look like a caravan, adorned with elaborate golden scrollwork, hand-painted lions and birds, and old-fashioned lettering. The sign read:

Tickets Sold Here
Good On Any Ride
Anytime
No Refunds

It reminded him of something from the first part of The Wizard of Oz, the black-and-white part. The teenage girl seated behind the plastic window with the hole in it looked bored, as though she'd rather be anywhere else (except maybe school). Chewing gum and wearing a so last year's shirt that read, "I'm with stupid," even though she sat by herself, she fixed her stare on Ranleigh.

"How many?" she seemed to sigh.

"What?" Ranleigh responded.

"Tickets. How many tickets do you want? I don't have all day, you know," she replied, which struck Ranleigh as odd because that's exactly what she did have. It was something kids did to appear older and tougher, adopting phrases without fully understanding them. And the older they grew, the more they did it. It's the same reason they took up smoking.

"Yes, umm, okay. Well, how does it work?" Stupid question. Ranleigh wanted to take it back as soon as it came out of his mouth. What he wanted to know was how many tickets would he need for the really good rides.

"Listen, kid," she said, blowing a large bubble-gum bubble and producing cracking sounds as she popped it back into her mouth.

Kid. That was rich. She was probably only four or five years older than Ranleigh, on the outside. She continued, "Rides like the Zipper, the Ferris Wheel, and the Scrambler will run you three tickets each. The Funhouse and the Antique Cars are two, and the kiddie rides..." She paused. "Are one. Got it?"

"Yeah, I got it," Ranleigh grumbled, feeling his face flush. "I'll take ten tickets."

"Ten, huh? Big spender!" She took his five-dollar bill, carefully detached a rectangle of perforated tickets from the main booklet and handed them back to Ranleigh along with his change. "Have fun, kid."

"Thanks," Ranleigh mechanically replied, although the last thing he felt like doing was thanking the ticket girl. He turned away from her, noticing a line had formed behind him consisting of families waiting for their turn at the window.

Ranleigh passed by a few midway games on the main strip of the Kinglin Rodeo, the whack-a-mole, the ring toss, and a dunk tank. The aggressive nature of the few carnies running the games made him feel nervous, so he pretended not to hear them. Which as a strategy, left much to be desired, as there was no one else around, and the carnies were shouting directly at him. Perhaps he could have pretended to be deaf, but he knew that wouldn't fool anyone.

He had already allocated his meagre funds for rides, popcorn, cotton candy, and if there was anything left, maybe a Coke. He wouldn't be playing any games this year. And besides, he never won the big prizes anyway.

Just past the ring toss, a middle-aged woman caught Ranleigh's attention. She appeared prim, proper and overdressed for the sunny weather but seemed pleasant enough, even if she looked a little crackers. Standing behind a large plexiglass cube that was about halfway filled with cardboard tickets, she offered him a friendly greeting.

"Good morning, honey. Care to buy a ticket? We're raising money to help the high school purchase better football uniforms. You look like you might play a little football yourself. Want to give it a try?" she proposed.

Standing in the middle of the midway lane, with Fleetwood Mac now playing over the loudspeaker, Ranleigh thought it over. He could hear the screams falling from the first rides of the day. Glancing over his shoulder at the cotton candy stand, he could almost feel the money burning in his pocket.

Unlike the carny games, this stuff wasn't rigged (a kid at school told him that you could never win the hit-the-balloon-with-a-dart game, because the darts were dull, and they under-inflated the balloons). And if he won, he would get some real money instead of some crappy stuffed animal. Maybe a lot of money. He felt the first flicker of excitement as he agonized over what to do. If he lost, he would have less to spend on junk food. But if he won... IF.

Come on, Ran. You know you want to. You're feeling lucky, right? Just because you never win anything doesn't mean shit. Somebody has to win, so why not you?

Yeah, but Grandma might question me on how I spent the money.

And if she's with Verna, I'll for sure get it worse. Christians aren't keen on gambling, and I'll never hear the end of it.

Don't worry about Verna. She's fucking crazy. Take a chance, Ran. Take a chance for once in your life.

"What's it gonna be, honey? You want a ticket or not?" the lady asked.

"Sure. Sure, I'll do it. I'll take two, please." Ranleigh unfolded a dollar bill the girl from the booth had given back to him and handed it over.

"Super! The football team thanks you for your support." The lady opened the lid of the cube and plunged her arm deep inside, stirring it as if mixing a giant tub of cake batter. "Voila," she said, extending two tickets to Ranleigh. He snatched them away without a thank you.

Ranleigh had forgotten all about the rides as he stood there holding both tickets in his right hand. He felt a potent blend of guilt and excitement that he curiously wished to prolong. He looked up and noticed the sign for the FUNHOUSE. He had unintentionally wandered just outside the entrance. Searching for a quiet spot, Ranleigh spotted a narrow alleyway nestled between the funhouse and a long white trailer. Leaning against the trailer, he examined the first ticket.

Ranleigh peeled back the strip, revealing two cowboy boots and a red pepper. Nothing. With a trembling index finger, he dug into the second tab and pulled it back. Still nothing. Doubt began to creep in.

Shake it off, Ran. You have three more chances on this ticket and a full five on the next one. He tore back the third and fourth tabs. Neither strip was a winner.

Please, God. Just let me win. Just this one time.

The fifth tab peeled off. Another loser. Ranleigh felt a suffocating wave of despair well up in his throat.

That's all right, Ran. That was just the warm-up for the main event. This is the ticket. The BIG ONE. He had never won anything back home, so why he believed he could win now was beyond him. Pulling back the top tab of the second ticket, he revealed nothing. A new kind of anger kindled in his belly. He was on the verge of discarding the remaining tabs just for spite when he witnessed a miracle, two cowboy boots and a bottle of hot sauce with a red arrow running through them like an electric current. He saw the arrow first.

He had won something. He feverishly flipped the ticket over and checked the legend. Ranleigh Meeks had won fifty dollars.

After collecting his winnings and a reluctant congratulations from the cake tub lady, Ranleigh needed to walk. He needed to calm down but having this money in his pocket awakened something within him. He felt electric. *He won he won he won.*

Ranleigh burned through the first set of ride tickets fast, running up and down the midway. When he finished, he went back and got more. He unraveled large swaths of candy floss, gorged himself on hot dogs and popcorn, and downed can after can of Coke. He didn't care if anyone was watching. But someone was.

"Hey kid, where's the fire?"

CHAPTER 5

SUNDAY, JUNE 24, 1979, 2:48 AM

Joe Parsons hadn't heard the ringing, but his wife sure had. A sharp, cold, bony elbow jolted him awake. She found it hysterical to jab him while he slept, making him think he was having a heart attack or just plain being attacked by someone who had broken into the house while he was sleeping peacefully in his bed. Her choice to jab him in such vulnerable moments made him think she was crazy. He figured he had a few more of these left before he genuinely had a heart attack, and the thought was a welcome one. Anything to get away from her.

She dropped the receiver on his face with that self-satisfied, shit-eating grin of hers, that said, *If I have to get up for this shit, then you do too, buddy-boy.* Well, mission accomplished, psycho. He was definitely up.

"Yeah. What?" He barked into the phone.

"Joe? Joe, listen, it's Sam," the voice said. "A call came in. House fire. Just getting going, so we should move. Might be able to stop it from getting to the other houses. See you at the station." The line went dead.

Joe rested his free palm on his forehead and half-hoped his wife might return the phone to its cradle as he handed it back over his shoulder. Nothing. So, Joe dropped the receiver beside him on the bed and sat up. Once the disconnected beeping started, he'd be well on his way, sending her flying into a rage. The thought of it would keep a smile on his face for the drive to the fire hall.

Taking the stairs two at a time, still in his pyjamas, Joe was careful not to wake his daughter, who was sleeping soundly in the next room. His wife never bothered asking where he was going or when he'd be back, but if his daughter woke up and he was gone, she would worry. As he closed the front door behind him, he could hear the first beeps emitting from the telephone receiver and smiled.

The roads were deserted. Joe's eyes had been rapidly deteriorating since his fortieth birthday and were not much good in the dark. Despite his poor eyesight, he was still the best driver in the department. Although this was strictly a volunteer gig, he had a natural feel for handling the big engines. Because of this, when he was on rotation, the other firefighters would never consider taking the helm. The one thing the volunteer fire brigade was consistently commended for was their lightning response time. None of the other volunteers were willing to risk that standing for a shot at first chair. Joe found it amusing that you could make a heaping, shit pile of mistakes at the scene of a fire, just as long as you arrived on time.

There hadn't been a night call in a long time. Joe kept meaning to get his eyes looked at, but he had put it off. He knew that new glasses would have to go on his wife's insurance. He didn't know if they would still be sharing the same bed, let alone the same insurance policy when it came time to submit the request. The last thing he needed was to be stuck with a bill for an otherwise useless pair of eyeglasses, so he had held off. And besides, his grandfather had been diagnosed with glaucoma and that was something he wasn't ready to face. When Joe arrived at the station, Sam was already suited up and Engine No. 1 was running.

As Joe climbed out of his car and ran past Sam through the light mist that cooled the warmth on his cheeks, he shouted over the loud rumbling of the truck, "How did you get here so fast?"

"I wasn't sleeping," Sam shouted back. Joe was concerned and knew they would have to have a heart-to-heart later. This conversation had been coming for a long time. When you were on the graveyard rotation, you had to keep the drinking under control. The Fire Marshal would turn a blind eye to a beer or two with supper, but not more than that.

Sam checked the address again. He had scrawled it on an envelope and was half-cut when he took it down. For the most part, Sam liked the volunteer gig. He liked working with Joe all right, but Joe moved too slow. Joe was carrying an extra sixty pounds, mostly around the gut, but he could maneuver that bitch of a truck better than anyone could.

They hadn't been out on a call together for a good while. Sam figured it to be a month or so. The last one was a minor deal. Some kids had started a bonfire down at the lake, and it was going pretty good when a kid misjudged his footing, tipped over, and fell right in. Minor burns. Fire out. Party over. But tonight was different, and they needed to move. Shit. Why tonight? The one night he had decided to go out and knock back a few at The Bison's Head. Well, okay, more than a few, but a guy's entitled to do what he wants on his own time, right? Sam was just lucky that he hadn't brought that blonde from the bar home. He might have missed the call altogether.

Sam gave the horn a blast as Joe opened the driver's side door. "Jesus! I'm coming, already." Joe settled in quickly, flipped on the red and blue flashers, and pulled Engine No. 1 away from the station. He could smell the booze.

"Where we headed?" Joe asked, squinting.

Sam strained to read his own writing and was slow to respond. "Kinglin. 14 Kramden Avenue. The operator said it was the Hewitt house. Any idea?" On a regular drive, if you kept it close to the speed limit, Kinglin was about twenty minutes from Fairlawn City. Joe figured he could get there in ten. Twelve on the outside.

"The Hewitt house, huh?" Joe said, still squinting.

"Yeah, you know it?"

"Well, I know of it. Verna Hewitt lives in that house if she's still kicking. You know her. Everybody knows Verna. Her old man built that house, and if you ask her, he built the house and the town, and everything in between, back when they were still using pails for fires. You've seen her at a few of the department fundraisers. She parades herself around like some kind of royalty and expects to be treated as such. Well, karma's a bitch, I guess." Joe paused long enough to wonder what karmic debt he was paying off by still being saddled with that old bat back at home. Shifting his thoughts back to Verna Hewitt, Joe frowned. "And boy, is she gonna be pissed."

Sam reached into the side panel for the map book, shuffling some folders, call sheets, and instruction manuals around but came up empty.

"Shit!"

"What?"

"It's not here. That new kid on the day rotation must have taken it. Mentioned he was heading out for the weekend with that new girlfriend of his. Fucking idiot." As the implications of not having a map began to dawn on them, Sam started to sober right up. Hair of the dog? Fuck that. All you need is one hearty, mainline injection shot of pure adrenaline to get you to the church on time.

"Okay. Okay, Sam. We'll just go by street signs. I've done this before. Kinglin is small, and the streets were constructed on basically a grid. Once we pick up the general direction of the fire, we'll find the sign for Kramden. No problem. Besides, I've been through there a few times myself and may have a rough idea. 14, you said?" This was going to be tricky.

"Yep," Sam said.

Joe shook his head and smiled again. "Boy, she's gonna be really pissed," he said, gunning Engine No. 1.

CHAPTER 6

SATURDAY, JUNE 23, 1979, 12:05 PM

"Hey kid, where's the fire?" the voice barked in a deep, gravelly timbre. "Hey, kid. I'm talking to you."

Ranleigh spun around and saw what appeared to be a real-life cowboy leaning against a tent pole. The bingo tent was across from the funhouse. Ranleigh hadn't played yet but planned to head there next.

The cowboy looked old, though not nearly as old as Grandma or Verna. He wore a brown, lightly dusted hat, jeans, a leather vest over a plaid shirt, and scuffed cowboy boots. One of the boots had been taped up with grey duct tape. His bushy, grey mustache did not seem out of place, it was after all 1979. When he smiled the moustache straightened and reminded Ranleigh of the flat end of a straw broom.

Being addressed so directly slowed Ranleigh's thoughts a little and forced him to focus. Looking back at the cowboy and pointing his right index finger square at the middle of his chest, he said, "Who, me?"

"Yeah, kid. You. Where's the fire?"

"I don't know. I'm not sure what you mean," Ranleigh said.

His sugar high had crested. He was coming back down to earth. The feeling was not entirely unpleasant. It was like coming out of a dream combined with receiving a sharp elbow to the ribs.

"No fire, mister. Just in a hurry, I guess. See, I'm late."

The cowboy shrugged. "Didn't look much like that to me," he paused, and it was a long one.

It occurred to Ranleigh that cowboys were much the same in real life as they were on TV. They always took a long time to say anything, and this one was no different.

"I'm not due in the pen for another twenty minutes or so. First ride of the day. Thought I'd take in the sights. Not much to see that I haven't seen a thousand times all across the country, but you'd have to be as blind as a mole to miss you tearing all over God's green acre here. What gives, kid? Thought you might need a minute or two and catch your breath."

The cowboy lit a cigarette. Ranleigh stood frozen, his mind searching for a way to escape the intense gaze of the cowboy and slip back to the colourful chaos of the midway. At that moment, a group of rowdy teenagers swaggered by. Their cheap vinyl jackets creaked with each step, their stringy hair clung to their pimply faces, and they emitted a pungent odour of sweat and cigarettes. The leader recognized the cowboy.

"Look, boys. It's Dallas Cooper. *The* Dallas Cooper." The boys came to a halt and turned. The cowboy looked at the boy like one might look at a stray dog crossing the street.

Teen no. 1 said, "Dallas Cooper? No shit. Thought you was dead. Hey Dallas, how's it hanging?"

Teens no. 3 and no. 4 circled, standing shoulder to shoulder with their friends.

"Say, boys, a real-life, billy-from-the-hills, cousin-marrying cowboy," said the boy in front.

The brazen insult put the rest of the boys on edge. Dallas Cooper took a final, absentminded draw on his cigarette, and sighed out a last stream of smoke, never taking his eyes off the boy in front. He looked like a man familiar with such situations, and the weariness etched on his face suggested that he had long ago grown tired of them. Bone tired.

He offered Ranleigh a weary smile and said, "Howdy, fellas. Feeling no pain today, I see. Listen, just keep moving right along, or I might take up the notion to find your daddies and tell them all about the bong I saw you passing around in the parking lot." Expressions mutated from cool to scared, all except the boy in front who never flinched. He had grown accustomed to the frequent beatings his father dished out, which had only intensified since his mother left and took his sister with her.

"Listen, I don't give a shit what you do. I've seen enough of you peckerwoods over the years. And in the end, it always comes out the same. Unemployment, petty theft, in and out of AA meetings, and that's if you're lucky. Beating on your kin cause your daddy taught you well, and always looking backwards at the good old days. So why don't you take a walk, while I talk with my friend here?"

Ranleigh could see that the boy in front was working himself up, fists clenched, ready to shoot his mouth off again when a drunk stumbled around the busy carny stalls, a short distance off. As he pressed towards them with a sideways gait, his voice thundered and sputtered. He was a spitting image of the boy in the front.

"Brad, that you? Brad, get your sorry ass over here and take your whooping like a man, goddammit! What are you playing at?"

As Brad and the other boys disappeared down the nearest aisle, they left a cloud of dust and a parting remark, "We'll be seeing you around, Dallas."

"Well, kid. I'd best be going. They're expecting me in the pen. I would probably steer clear of those boys for the rest of the day, mind. Nice chewing the fat with you."

"Yes, you too, Mister Cooper." Ranleigh suddenly had the urge to ask if he could tag along.

"Call me Coop," the cowboy said as he tipped his hat back, pulled out another cigarette, and lit it.

"Okay, Coop."

"Didn't catch your name, kid?"

"Ranleigh."

"Ranleigh, huh?"

Ranleigh blushed.

"Well, Ranleigh. I'm off. Hey, if you're interested in seeing what it looks like when a grown man gets thrown around like a rag doll, I'm due to ride the orneriest horse in the province this afternoon. And if I don't break my neck doing it, I stand to make a good bit of money. If you're not too busy, that is?" Dallas Cooper was already making his way to the pavilion.

"No, sir. I mean, no sir, Coop. I'm not too busy at all," Ranleigh yelled after him. And that's how Ranleigh Meeks ended up holding the hand of a dying cowboy.

CHAPTER 7

SATURDAY, JUNE 23, 1979, 11:04 PM

Bradley and his friends felt secure under the cover of darkness. The cars parked earlier in the grassy field had begun to thin out, and the prairie night stretched out endlessly in every direction. It was a formless space, comforting and concealing. A shroud that hid the boys from the world.

Bradley, the leader of the group, was feeling good. The hits from the homemade bong were going down smoothly tonight. That he was their leader was a fact. Since the first grade, only one challenger had dared to take him on. But his response had been swift and savage, dissuading any others from making a similar miscalculation. He spent six months at a reform school in the city for that one and the boy had lost an eye for his trouble. But lately, the role of being their leader had been weighing him down.

It had become increasingly difficult for him to come up with things for them to do. Most of the time, they simply hung out, smoking weed, stealing his dad's car, and shooting his guns into the prairie (but only after the old man had passed out). The occasional visiting rodeo broke some of the monotony, but even those had become stale. He felt tense and restless.

With practically the whole town attending the rodeo, he felt like he had more eyes on him than ever. He had been lucky enough to avoid his father when he squared off with that broken-down old cowboy and managed to keep out of sight. But eventually, he would have to go home, and the thought of another beating fell over him like a dark sack.

"Hey Brad, what should we do now?" Teen no. 3 exhaled, his words whistling out and floating away with the bong smoke.

"Fuck off, freak," Brad snapped back. "Why is it always me who has to think of everything? Me. Me. Me. Why don't you morons come up with something to do for a change?"

"How about heading back to the dance? Don't think they've played Stairway to Heaven yet. I saw Shelley Whitmore there. She's easy," suggested teen no. 2.

"What? You think you'd have a chance with Shelley? You're dreaming. Maybe next life, and not with that pizza face of yours," Brad hissed.

Teen no. 3 chimed in, "Yeah, I'll take a large, hold the cheese."

After having his suggestion not to mention his self-worth shot down in flames, teen no. 2 could only muster, "Pass that over, you idiot," grabbing for the bong.

"Hang on, I'm not done."

"Fuck you, idiots!" Brad exploded, causing them to recoil. A family stopped momentarily to see what the commotion was, but deciding it was nothing out of the ordinary for a Saturday night in Kinglin, finished loading a blue speckled, Styrofoam cooler into the trunk of their car.

"I'm tired of this shit. It's the same thing every day with you flakes. *Brad, what are we gonna do today? Brad, can you score some more reefer? Brad, can you shake my pecker for me, I'm done?* Well, let me tell you something. I'm done. Hand it over, I'm going home."

He grabbed the bong from teen no. 3's hands, spilling a

dollop of dirty water down the front of his filthy Pink Floyd t-shirt. Then, he turned and headed back toward town.

As Brad reached the highway, he could hear the other boys calling after him.

"Come on, Brad... Stick around."

"Yeah, we'll figure something out."

"Maybe go back to the midway?"

All of which loosely translated to, *please don't go, Brad, and if you must go, leave your drugs.*

Just as Brad was crossing the midpoint of the empty highway, ready to turn and give those idiots a double-finger fuck-you, an idea struck him like a thunderbolt. He was inspired, reminiscent of the Christmas cartoon he had watched as a kid, the one about that green guy who hated Christmas. He too had an idea, didn't he? Brad shouted to them through the prairie wind, and they followed like they always did.

"Just shut up and walk," Brad hissed, hurrying them along the road.

The only potential roadblock in his plan turned out to be a non-issue. Worried that his dad might have come home early from the beer garden, which would have blown everything, Brad hesitated outside the garage. But the old man was nowhere in sight, and if he hadn't returned by now, he wouldn't be back for a long while. Maybe the old drunk was lying dead in some ditch along the highway, but Brad didn't have that kind of luck.

Getting the toolbox had been smooth sailing. Brad ordered one of the boys to carry it, but the rusty red box banged against his shins with every step, making one hell of a racket.

"Shut up."

"Sorry, Brad. It's pretty heavy. I need to use both hands."

"That's what my girlfriend said," teen no. 3 snickered.

"Then be a man and keep quiet. As I was saying, I think the whole town is probably still at the rodeo, but you never know. Like that new kid and his grandmother, they're probably home by now."

"Okay, Brad. Doing my best." One of the other boys in

Brad's crew let out a stoner's laugh. Brad grunted under his breath. He felt much better, but he would never let them know that.

"I gotta hand it to you, man. This is the single best idea you've ever had, and you've had some doozies, all right. Where did you come up with it, anyway? I mean, stealing one street sign or maybe two, that's okay. We've all done that. But all of them? The whole town in one shot? Genius. Pure genius."

Brad grinned a broad, I'm-king-shit smile, and put a hand up to stop them. Brad had a flair for the dramatic when the mood struck him.

"Well, Timmy, I'm glad you asked that question. I can't be certain on what day this particular idea came to me since I have ideas all the time. But when I thought of this one, I knew it was special. It must have come to me in the last week or so, and I was just keeping it in reserve for an evening like this. *AND KEEP THAT FUCKING TOOLBOX QUIET!* Now, where was I? Oh yeah, well, it occurred to me that we could take a sign or two, that would be good but not great. And considering that the town council, and that old bat Verna Hewitt, finally spent some money and replaced all the signs this spring, I thought it would piss them off if ALL of them were stolen. And because they're new, we could probably get them off quickly," Brad said.

"Genius," Timmy repeated, laughing. "Get them off."

"Okay, boys, this shouldn't take too long," Brad motioned them over. They stood directly below the street sign that would have directed Joe and Sam to the Hewitt fire and if the sign had been there, Verna Hewitt might have survived.

Two boys held the ladder and hoisted the toolbox up to Timmy, while Brad grinned and lit a smoke.

CHAPTER 8

SUNDAY, JUNE 24, 1979, 2:40 AM

As the glow grew from a dim amber to a bright dirty yellow, it illuminated the figure sprinting down the road. The horses had gone into a state of full-tilt panic, trapped in the enclosed space with the suffocating scent of smoke coating the insides of their moist nostrils. This was the scent of *GET OUT*. The solitary horse appeared to understand the meaning of the smell: they needed to get to a larger space than their current confinement. Safety and death eluded his understanding—concepts forever beyond his grasp. But fear, fear he knew. And when fear struck, he instinctively sought the biggest space within reach.

Instinctively, the solitary horse turned his hindquarters towards the gate, snorted out a warning, and began to back up. Sensing he was close enough, he delivered a forceful kick with both hind legs, attempting to move the gate. The gate resisted, remaining shut. The inside thing that grasped his fear urged him to try again, and he did. This time, he unleashed a powerful kick. A resounding snap reached his ears, and he sensed his world would soon be bigger.

The other horses observed him but failed to understand.

One of them started kicking at nothing, thrashing the air and lashing out at the scent. *Scent kicker.* The horse squealed. Despite exhaustion, others continued their cacophony of awful noises, galloping back and forth along the length of the pen, a mere twenty feet, some colliding with their companions.

A smaller white horse with brown spots ventured too close to the *scent kicker* and met with the explosive force of a hoof, shattering her upper leg near the elbow. She collapsed heavily, struggling to lift her head out of harm's way amidst the flurry of hooves. Witnessing the commotion, the solitary horse felt the urge to rush towards her aid but pressed on with his mission at the gate. Almost free. He seemed to grasp that by reaching the larger space, the others might follow. He left the injured white horse where she lay and, with one final kick, broke free from the enclosure. And he was out.

CHAPTER 9

SUNDAY, JUNE 24, 1979, 2:58 AM

Dallas Cooper grimaced in agony as he hobbled toward the blazing house, his broken arm throbbing with sharp pains. Finding the house took longer than expected for two reasons. Firstly, his arm injury rendered driving impossible, forcing him there on foot. Secondly, he didn't know the house's precise location, relying on rising smoke signals above Kinglin's rooftops as his guide. Eventually, he arrived at the inferno and caught sight of a spectral figure, a woman dressed in a sheer white nightgown, perched on a neighbouring porch.

The woman in white perpetually teetered on the edge, prone to nervous breakdowns driven by her relentless concern for the safety of herself and others. Raised in a family where danger lurked around every corner, she developed a vigilant stance to avoid harm. However, tragedy struck during her teenage years when a devastating house fire took her younger brother and left her mother with lifelong, disfiguring burns. The experience gave rise to an obsession with safety within the woman. She purchased the first smoke detector when it hit the market in 1965 and equipped each floor of her house with brass fire extinguishers. Sleep never came easy as she kept a watchful eye on her neighbour's residences. So, when she saw smoke rising from Verna's house, she sprang into action.

"Have you called it in?" Cooper shouted.

"Oh my God, yes. I got the operator a few minutes ago. Is she out? Did she get out?"

"I haven't seen anyone come out. Are there children in there? Do any kids live in the house?"

"No! Just Ms. Hewitt. She would be alone. Oh, God. You haven't seen her?" The woman yelled back, oblivious to the wind from the fire blowing her nightgown against her body, revealing too much, but she didn't notice.

"I'll check around back," Coop said, making a run for the backyard. He didn't catch all of what the woman said next but thought he heard her yell something about Ms. Hewitt never being out this late.

Black smoke billowed through shattered back windows, casualties of the raging heat. Awful sounds of cracking, popping, and groaning were coming from within the house, yet no screams or calls for help could be heard. Where was the goddamn fire department?

Navigating the perimeter of the burning house, Cooper's vision blurred amid the suffocating smoke. Then, he caught sight of something that initially did not seem real, attributing it to his earlier head injury. Ranleigh Meeks was coming towards him, leading the very horse that had thrown Cooper earlier that day.

Cooper tightly closed his eyes for a moment, trying to clear his vision, but the acrid smoke burned too much. He tried to swallow a breath but couldn't, the stifling air denied him. An impulse to shake his head arose, but he resisted, fearing his brain might come loose and slosh around inside his skull.

"Coop! Coop!" Through the pounding ache in his head and the haze of smoke clouding his eyes, Ranleigh's voice pierced through the chaos, calling out to him.

CHAPTER 10

SATURDAY, JUNE 23, 1979, 12:30 PM

Ranleigh trailed behind Dallas Cooper. Cooper moved like he didn't have a care in the world, as if he could easily brush away anything that got in his way, like swatting away a horsefly.

Dallas Cooper had been a rodeo cowboy since his youth. At 52 years old, he was one of the circuit's oldest riders, but retirement was out of the question for him. The thrill of the rodeo had been driving him since he left his small farm town to join the circuit. Aware that his days were numbered, he had to admit that his aging body wasn't what it used to be, and the injuries were becoming more frequent and took longer to heal. The broken bones, torn ligaments, and concussions made it difficult to think straight some days. Despite it all, he loved the camaraderie with his fellow cowboys and the fans who gathered to watch him compete.

"Hey kid, hurry up if you're coming. They'll be waiting for me, and I still need to get my gear on and saddle up," Cooper said.

Ranleigh tried picking up the pace, but he was exhausted. His mind still spun from the rush of his gambling win, but now overshadowed by the fear of running into his grandmother or Verna. The sun beat down on him, making him feel like he was walking through a furnace. Sweat trickled down his back, causing his Mork and Mindy shirt to cling uncomfortably to his skin. It was unusually hot for this early in the summer.

The rodeo roared in his ears. Hooves pounded the dirt, cheers and whoops erupted from the crowd, the clanking of metal gates and the loud distorted announcer's voice scratching through cone-shaped speakers cut through the din. Anxiously scanning the faces for signs of his grandmother, Ranleigh shielded his eyes with his arm, partially hiding his face.

"Hey kid, what's eatin' ya?" Ranleigh normally did a pretty good job of hiding what he felt, but clearly, Coop could see into him more than most. Perhaps Cooper just cared enough to look. Still, Ranleigh attempted to deflect his concern.

"I'm fine," Ranleigh said.

"That so?"

"Yeah," Ranleigh replied, his gaze still fixed on the crowd, vigilant for any sign of his grandmother.

"Kid, you haven't been 'fine' since I saw you running around earlier," Cooper said.

Ranleigh felt a twinge of unease as if he'd been caught eavesdropping or stealing. Surveying the fairground, he felt a mix of relief and disappointment as the rides and booths had returned to their mundane state, no longer gateways to other dimensions or rockets destined for Mars.

"Listen, nothing can be all that bad, right?" Dallas Cooper motioned for Ranleigh to join him on a nearby bench.

Seated beside the cowboy, Ranleigh asked, "Aren't you going to be late?"

"Look, if you have something to say, then I'm gonna wager it must be pretty important. I'm all ears, kid. They'll wait for me."

From the bothered mind of a nine-year-old Ranleigh confessed.

"I was supposed to meet my grandma for lunch, but I didn't show up," his eyes fixed on his Kodiak boots. "I'm afraid she'll be mad and probably worried. She's here with her friend Ms. Hewitt, who doesn't like me much." He hesitated, glancing back at the rodeo arena. "I want to stay and watch the rest of the rodeo, but if I run into my grandma, she'll drag me back home. I was planning to hide out and deal with it later."

Ranleigh looked up at his companion, his expression troubled. "But when I won that money and was riding the rides and eating all the junk food, it was like... I don't know, I didn't care about her or anything else."

Cooper listened intently but interrupted Ranleigh before he could finish.

"Listen here, Ranleigh. My old man, he was a drinker. It messed him up real bad, rotted his brain from the inside out. He tried going to AA, but it never took. I even drove him there a couple of times myself and learned a thing or two. I learned that drinkers love the way booze makes them feel, but like I said, it messes you up real bad in the end. You don't want that for yourself. You're a good kid. Understand?" Ranleigh nodded, although he didn't fully grasp the warning. "And it starts with lying," Dallas added.

Once again, Ranleigh nodded. He wasn't sure what Cooper was getting at with his warning, but it felt important. It made him think of the lottery ticket, wondering if Cooper knew something he didn't.

"I don't know, kid," Dallas said, scratching his chin. "Grandmothers are a funny bunch. They practically invented forgiveness. Christians may claim it but don't believe it, it was grandmothers. I remember when I was your age, I got into all sorts of trouble. But no matter how bad I messed up, my grandma always made me feel like everything was gonna be all right." He paused, taking a deep drag from his cigarette. "Let's go find that grandmother of yours. I bet she's worried sick."

It was over in an instant. Ranleigh's digital watch read twelve seconds. He had timed it for fun. But those twelve seemingly endless seconds stretched out before him, like the prairie.

Dallas Cooper lay face down in the dirt, not moving. The two men who had brought the quarter horse to the pen minutes earlier rushed toward Cooper, waving their hats and yelling to prevent the horse from trampling the fallen cowboy. The once lively crowd fell silent, after letting out a collective gasp but before leaping to their feet in anticipation. They now remained frozen in place, except for Verna Hewitt, who remained seated, steadfast in her Vernaness. The horse eventually lost interest in the men and wandered off.

Ranleigh had been strategically placed between his grandmother and Ms. Hewitt, keeping him on an invisible but short leash. He disliked the way Verna's leg spilled over her seat, rubbing against his.

He was in trouble for sure, but things didn't unfold nearly as badly as he had expected. The silver lining was being allowed to stay for the rest of the rodeo, an act of mercy he now regretted. The sole reason his grandmother hadn't immediately taken him home as punishment for his tardiness was that there was no way Verna Hewitt was *not* going to be seen in her prime seat in the bleachers for all to see.

The hotdog his grandmother had purchased for him for lunch lay abandoned and half-eaten beside his left foot. He didn't remember dropping it during the incident. Looking from Cooper to the ketchup-smeared hotdog and back again, he felt sick.

The two men rolled Cooper onto his back, one of them retrieving something small from his breast pocket and pushing it beneath Cooper's nose. After a few seconds, the cowboy let out a loud groan and attempted to sit up. The men restrained him, yelling at him to stay put. Another groan escaped Cooper's lips. Then, "Get me up! Get me up, goddammit!" He wheezed.

Ranleigh wasn't certain if everyone in the crowd had heard Cooper's words as clearly as he did, but the scattered applause indicated that enough of them had. As the two younger men helped Cooper into a sitting position, applause began to spread like wildfire through the remaining audience. Once they got him on his feet, clapping transformed into resounding cheers. The people of Kinglin had undoubtedly received their money's worth that day. Had they ever.

The cowboy was injured; that was obvious. A deep gash on his forehead bled, resembling war paint, and something seemed wrong with his arm. When one of the men attempted to lend support, Cooper recoiled from what looked like an electric shock. After a few more steps, he regained his balance and stood, facing the crowd. Once he steadied himself, he removed his hat with his good hand and waved it in the air, eliciting even louder cheers. The spectators had forgotten about the horse entirely.

Ranleigh's nine-year-old mind struggled to process the event he had just witnessed. The violence of it looked nothing like the fake stunts on TV. His thoughts had been fragmented, they had raced through his mind like disjointed writing, akin to words on a telegram he had once seen in a history book.

TELEGRAM

cowboy smoking a cigarette (stop) Twelve seconds (stop) Horse arriving in the pen, appearing agitated (stop) Horse trampling the cowboy (stop) Cowboy's hand stuck in the rein (stop) 8 seconds (stop) Horse attempting to throw the rider (stop) I like hotdogs (stop) 4 seconds (stop) Cowboy has things under control (stop) Cowboy waving hat (stop) Oh my God, he's not moving (stop) Cowboy is down (stop) Ketchup and mustard, please (stop) Ketchup and blood (stop) Please send help! (stop) (stop) (stop) (stop)

CHAPTER 11

SUNDAY, JUNE 24, 1979, 3:12 AM

As Joe Parsons pushed Engine No. 1 down the highway, the town of Kinglin came into view. The cool, damp air carried a faint scent of burning paper, and the distant glow of flames illuminated the sky. Most of the houses stood dark, their windows reflecting the flicker of fire. Joe felt relieved that news of the fire hadn't spread yet. The last thing he wanted was to collide with a rubbernecker who had wandered into the middle of the street for a better view.

Joe turned to his partner and said, "Sam, you can hit the siren now. We don't want some drunk out for a late-night stroll stumbling into the road." Sam, lost in the sight of the smoke, didn't respond.

Joe repeated, "Sam, the siren. Now." Sam flicked the switch, and the banshee wail of the siren pierced the air, echoing across the Great Plain, sending prairie dogs scurrying into their burrows. Joe thought of his wife.

"What was that address again?" Joe asked as he maneuvered the truck through the dark streets of Kinglin. If Ranleigh had stayed put, he would have witnessed the fire truck roaring past his grandmother's front porch.

"14 Kramden," Sam replied. Joe slowed the rig and steered it in the direction of the fire. They had made good time, but without a map, they risked losing their advantage.

"Sam, keep your eyes on that smoke and see if you can get us close," Joe said, focusing on the road.

Sam nodded and leaned forward, attempting to get a better view over the rooftops. "Sure. I mean, yes. Okay," he said.

Joe added, "I'll check the signs, and once we get onto Kramden, we'll be as good as there."

Approaching the next corner, Joe scanned the area for street signs but couldn't spot any. He turned to Sam and asked, "I'm not seeing any street signs. Maybe my eyes. You?"

"No, I didn't. But keep going straight, and we'll find it."

A memory flashed in front of Joe, projecting itself onto the windshield like a hologram. It was a memory of his daughter getting lost in the Fairlawn City Mall. She couldn't have been more than four at the time. Joe had taken his daughter and wife to the mall and suggested they wait for his wife in the food court to avoid dragging his daughter through countless stores. He had only taken his eyes off of her for a second but in that brief moment, she had wandered off. He searched frantically, checking exits and scanning the crowd for any sign of her. Panic set in, freezing him in place.

Forcing himself to move, running up the down escalator, two steps at a time, to the upper level and checking every store entrance and person with a child. It wasn't until he looked over the railing at the fountain on the main floor that he spotted her, sitting there eating her ice cream cone. His knees almost gave out.

"No signs!" Joe yelled. Sam, too absorbed in the smoke, didn't think he had heard correctly.

"What?" he said.

Pointing, Joe said, "Not there! Not there or there or there." As Sam's eyes searched the same pole Joe had examined seconds earlier, "Bullshit!"

The calm in Joe's voice vanished as he swung the truck up

and drove through the signless streets. "Let's try the next block," he said.

"Get that horse back and away from the fire, son," Coop said, biting down on the pain he sounded testy.

The boy had somehow managed to get hold of the horse that had thrown him and made his way to the fire. The siren's sound was growing louder. Again. Coop had heard it when he spotted the boy and the horse heading his way. At that moment, he wasn't sure which provided more relief, for himself, the boy, and the horse, or for Ms. Hewitt, the sound of the approaching firetruck.

Assuming the truck would be arriving momentarily, Coop had shifted gears, figuring out how to get the horse back in the paddock with his arm the way it was. If this one managed an escape, the others would likely find a way out too, potentially putting an end to the rodeo for the entire season. *Dammit.*

But the firetruck never arrived. It had sounded close and then appeared to be moving away. That was impossible. Why the hell would they turn around? Maybe he was hearing things. Too many kicks to the head? Perhaps the wail of the siren had tricked his ears into believing it was moving away from the flames. But if that were the case, the rescue truck should have arrived by now. From the sound of it, they couldn't be more than three blocks away, yet they remained nowhere in sight.

A crowd had gathered. The sound of hushed whispers and murmurs could be heard among the group, with occasional gasps from those closest to the flames. Some were dressed in formal pyjamas, while others, mostly teenaged girls, wore t-shirts that were too short, the Fonz or Farrah Fawcett-Majors stenciled on the front. The neighbour in white returned to her front porch, now wearing a bathrobe. Amidst the chaos, a strange sense of solidarity emerged amongst the onlookers, as if they were united in prayer for a miracle.

"Listen, kid. Get that horse away from the house, will ya? There's no telling what he might do, especially when that damn firetruck arrives with the siren blaring. If, it ever arrives."

Ranleigh followed the command and tried to pull the horse back down the street, but the horse refused to budge.

"Come on, boy!" Ranleigh pulled on the bridle with all his strength. Coop shifted his complete attention back to the fire. *Come on, fellas. There's a woman in there, for fuck's sake. We're over here*, Coop thought as he glanced at the side of the house. The fire was spreading.

We're over here. We're over here. Over here. The phrase played over and over in his mind like that wartime song from his childhood. Over there, over there. Send the word, send the word over there. Then it hit him. *THEY DON'T KNOW WHERE WE ARE! FOR SOME REASON, WHATEVER MISTAKE. THEY CAN'T FIND US!* He addressed the onlookers:

"Listen up! Everybody, listen up! I don't think the fire department knows where we are, or at least the guys in the truck don't. I think they're going around in circles, chasing their tails. Don't ask me how I know. I just do." The crowd seemed to accept his reasoning. "So, here's what we're gonna do. We have to let them know we're here. And loud. But shouting and screaming probably won't help things, probably just bounce all over these streets. So, my young friend here, Ranleigh, is going to lead us in a good old-fashioned singsong. A nice round of 'Row, Row, Your Boat.' And loud. Got it?" Some chuckled in disbelief as the neighbours shuffled in their slippers.

"Okay, kid? Got it? Nice and loud now."

Ranleigh faced the crowd.

Row, row, row your boat
Gently down the stream
Merrily, merrily, merrily, merrily
Life is but a dream

"Good. Again, kid. And keep it going. And folks, you're gonna have to do better than that. As loud as you can now."

Ranleigh started again. Coop removed his hat and gently placed it on Ranleigh's head. Watching the crowd and the boy, his right arm raised to conduct them, Coop knew then and there that the fire department would never make it on time.

"We must be close," Sam yelled back through the open window. Joe didn't hear him or couldn't be bothered to answer, too focused on finding a damn street sign. Any damn sign. Smoke seemed to be coming from one place, but when they thought they had a lock on it, the column of black vapour shifted direction as if coming from the opposite side of town. Every time Sam believed they were close, they would turn a corner only to reveal a row of sleepy houses, mocking him in their slumber. When he was on the verge of jumping out and tracking the fire on foot, he heard it.

Singing? Could that be right? He knew he had one too many earlier, but surely this call was sobering him up. An adrenaline rush couldn't make someone more intoxicated, could it? Rubbing his eyes and shaking his head, he strained to listen. It was singing, and the singing was getting louder.

"Joe, stop the truck. For Christ's sake, stop the truck and kill the siren."

Joe wasn't one to easily follow orders, just ask the wife, who could give you a laundry list of infractions dating back to the moon landing, but reluctantly, he obeyed his junior's command. The engine's growl cranked down into silence.

"Do you hear that? Do you hear it?" Sam asked. At first, Joe couldn't hear a thing and thought Sam was grasping. But as his ears adjusted to the silence, he heard it.

"That song the kids sing?" Joe said.

"Yep. Told you. Can't you hear it?" Sam pounded his fist on the dashboard. "They're telling us where they are." Joe didn't wait for Sam to finish. He started up Engine No. 1 and headed straight toward the Kinglin town choir.

As the truck rolled up to the scene, the crowd of neighbours let out a cheer. Ranleigh didn't join in. Just moments ago, he had seen Dallas Cooper make his way onto Verna's porch.

Ranleigh watched as the cowboy kicked in the front door, good arm raised like a shield. Coop ran into the burning house. Ranleigh wasn't sure how long he had been inside, and he wasn't sure what he could do to help his friend.

Two firemen jumped down from the cab of the truck. The younger one pulled a long hose off the side paneling, while the older one approached the crowd, asking them to back up and if anyone was in the house.

"Dallas Cooper and Ms. Verna Hewitt are in the house!" Ranleigh screamed. Joe turned to see a small boy holding the reins of a large brown horse.

"How long have they been in there?" Joe yelled, turning toward the kid. "How long?"

CHAPTER 12

SUNDAY, JUNE 24, 1979, 4:04 AM

Amidst the chaos, Ranleigh, Dallas Cooper, and the horse slipped away unnoticed. Coop, silent and pale, trembled alongside the boy as they shuffled along Main Street, crossed the railroad tracks, and reached the edge of the vast prairie. Ranleigh struggled under the weight of his friend, uncertain of how far they would be able to go. Coop's condition was deteriorating, and he frequently stopped to rest, each break longer than the last. Coop seemed determined to reach a destination he had in his mind, urging Ranleigh forward. Ranleigh considered asking but decided against it.

With every step, the silence deepened, and Ranleigh's damp pyjama bottoms clung to his ankles, itching them from the mud and grass. His arms ached from supporting Coop's weight. When Ranleigh bent down to scratch his itchy ankles, Coop lost his balance and fell. As Ranleigh tried to figure out his next move, the stallion approached Coop, lowering its head and nudging the cowboy.

Despite Ranleigh's attempts to pull the horse away, it refused to budge. Again, the stallion nudged Coop, prompting him to stir. With a terrible groan, Dallas Cooper rose to his feet, using the horse's shoulder for support. Coop struggled to hoist himself onto the horse's back. Incredibly, the horse did not resist, sensing something *ending*. Recognizing Coop's intention, Ranleigh offered what help he could. Ranleigh could see clearly that there would be no chance of getting Coop upright on the horse, so he yelled, "Coop! You're almost there. If you can, just lie across his back. If you can do that, we can get a lot further."

The cowboy seemed to understand and, with one excruciating lunge, managed to position himself across the horse's back.

"Good. That's a good boy," he murmured. Ranleigh wasn't sure if Coop addressed him or the horse, but it didn't matter. They continued their journey into the prairie, and darkness swallowed them whole, until Dallas Cooper, the rodeo king, passed out for good.

They trudged deeper into the prairie, the air carrying the scent of earth and wildflowers. The darkness consumed them, and Ranleigh struggled to make out the ground ahead for the next few steps. Twisting his ankles on slippery rocks the size and shape of prehistoric eggs, Ranleigh followed the horse's lead. He heard faint pops from the cracking of the cowboy's arm and the rhythmic swish of the horse's tail.

The moon cast no shadows. It felt like Mars. Glancing back, Ranleigh saw the town illuminated, tiny homes huddled together, they seemed to be warming themselves around the Hewitt bonfire. Ranleigh wished they were on Mars. We could establish a base camp and radio back to Earth. He imagined Mars Landing Basecamp Alpha, seeing himself from a distance, reminiscent of a paperback cover he had once taken down from his mother's bookshelf.

Yellowed pages with a scent of mothballs. On the cover of Mission to Mars, Ranleigh had seen a vivid image of the red planet's shadowed valley, where a boy led a horse and a man wearing a spacesuit and a fishbowl helmet. Studying the glossy cover, Ranleigh could almost feel the red sand under their boots. The image had always seemed like a distant dream until this moment as he trudged through the vast prairie with his weary companion, struggling to keep Dallas Cooper alive.

The movie screen appeared distant, too far away to feel real, and Ranleigh wondered if he might be dreaming. The gleaming white monolith floated in the darkness, prompting Ranleigh to wonder who would put a Drive-In all the way out here. Seeking shelter from the wind, the horse gravitated toward it.

Brad was mad. His once-inspired plan had devolved into the clusterfuck of all time, and he knew it was only a matter of time before they fingered him for the fire. That's what happens when you entrust the finer details to a bunch of chumps. Surely to God, no judge would sentence him for something like this. He had merely stolen a few street signs to break the monotony (well, okay, every street sign). He wasn't the one who started the fire, after all. You try living in this shithole year after year and not go completely out of your mind with boredom.

He sure as hell didn't mean to kill the old bitch. And, deep down, he knew that the town would sleep a little more soundly tonight, knowing they would never have to tolerate Verna Hewitt's bullshit again. Not in the grocery store, not in the supermarket, and certainly not in church on Sundays. Hell, they should give him a goddamn medal for putting her out of their misery.

Brad had been swinging on an old tire swing in his backyard (a patch of dirt, more like) drinking a beer when he caught a whiff of the smoke. His father still hadn't dragged his drunk ass home and Brad had still not decided what to do with the flatbed pick-up filled with stolen street signs. With nothing better to occupy his time he decided to check things out. Brad hopped off the tire swing, flicked the cigarette butt towards the side of the truck with one hand, and took another swig of beer with the other.

The scent of fire was all too familiar to Brad. Back in second grade, he went through a little pyromaniac phase. Newspapers were his thing, but not for reading. He would wake up early on Saturday mornings and snatch a few papers from the corner, waiting to be collected and distributed by the local paperboy. Once home, he would position himself between two garages, retrieve his collection of matchbooks, and start igniting them one by one. Something was captivating about the way the matchstick heads would burst into flames and catch in a row, releasing the sweet smell of sulphur that filled his young nostrils, making him feel powerful. The smell of burning newspaper pages differed from that of the matches—richer, reminiscent of oak. Brad enjoyed how the paper crinkled and curled up, almost like skin. The ashes held the shape of the page until a cool morning breeze scattered them away.

With a beer nestled between his legs, Brad turned the key in the ignition, slammed the stick into first gear, and sped off towards the sweet aroma of the burning house, taking a deep, refreshing breath. Locating the source of the smell proved easy, and Brad felt somewhat surprised to find the Hewitt house already engulfed in flames.

As he approached the scene, Brad slowed his father's truck to a crawl. A group of bystanders stood huddled on the sidewalk with their backs turned to the road, mouths agape. A fireman futilely attempted to extinguish the blaze while another crouched over a lumpy, uneven black body bag. Brad briefly entertained the idea of parking the truck in a nearby driveway to see if he could get a good look at what (or who) was inside the bag, but the sound of stolen signs rattling in the truck bed snapped him back and he quickly abandoned the idea.

Turning the truck away from the scene and towards the highway, Brad spotted three figures making their way deep into the prairie.

The Drive-In lay deserted. Ranleigh guided the horse through the aisles, maneuvering around the metal poles that cradled metal speakers. Aware that Cooper couldn't stand to go much further, Ranleigh steered them towards the playground nestled beneath the colossal movie screen, like a miniature child's toy.

"Ranleigh?" Coop whispered. "Where am I?"

"You're on the back of a horse, and we're on the planet Mars. We've been walking for a while now."

"Let me down, Ranleigh. Get me down."

Ranleigh had hoped to lead Coop to the snack bar for shelter from the wind, but the horse came to a stop near one of the many metal poles scattered throughout the parking area. After helping Coop down onto the gravel mound, Ranleigh tied the horse. Unsure of what to do next, Ranleigh settled down beside the cowboy and looked up at the movie screen. The soundtrack crackled through the metal speakers, and soon an image formed on the screen, an astronaut's face hovering over a gigantic clay egg, bobbing his head in curiosity. Ranleigh had seen the movie's commercial and recognized it. Ominous and deeply dark music blared through the speakers as the egg opened, and a creature leaped out, attaching itself to the spaceman's helmet.

Weaving along the highway, passing the pavilion and horse paddock, Brad squinted, closing one eye trying to focus. He could faintly make out the silhouettes making their way toward the Drive-In. Spotting the horse, he was reminded of that dumb kid and the cowboy, but his luck couldn't be that good.

Veering the truck off the highway and onto the prairie, Brad headed towards the Drive-In. Gotta admit he was somewhat surprised to see a movie playing on the screen. It was a film he had watched at least three times that June. People said it was terrifying, but Brad had been bored. Not even the scene where an alien burst out of this guy's chest during dinner had made him flinch. But hey, with nothing to do in Kinglin, he went back and watched it again, so he knew it like the back of his hand.

If he weren't so loaded, he might have noticed the conspicuous absence of cars and the fact that it was way too late for a movie to be running, even for a Drive-In. As Brad drew nearer, he could see that his earlier assumption about the figures huddled in a parking spot was right on, it was the cowboy and that fucking kid.

Struggling to focus, fury surged up from his stomach, settling in his head and pressing down on his eye sockets. They had made him look like a fool. His crew had seen it, and it had put him back on the old man's radar. If there was one thing Brad McGinnis despised, it was being humiliated. Pushing harder on the gas pedal, a current of memories flooded his mind, every teacher he had since the first grade, his cellmates at the reform school, that shrink they made him see when he knocked that kid's eye out. Everyone who had ever made him feel shame. These memories mixed with the rage behind his eyes, threatening to pop them right out of their sockets.

Settling on a swing set beneath the enormous screen, Ranleigh was plummeting into a full regression, swinging high and sucking his thumb, too exhausted to think clearly. Unaware of the truck's approach, he slowed the swing to a stop and absentmindedly kicked at the sand with the toe of his boot. Thoughts of getting help crossed his mind, but he knew Coop wanted nothing to do with doctors. Besides, he couldn't bring himself to leave him.

If not for the movie soundtrack blaring through the speakers, Ranleigh might have heard the truck, but he didn't. When he finally looked up, it was too late. The headlights of the pickup danced like fireflies in the darkness. Before he could jump off the wooden swing seat, the rest of the truck came into view. The driver swerved erratically, mud and grass spurting from the tires. The driver attempted to regain control. Ranleigh wanted to run to the horse and his friend, to warn them and get them out of harm's way, but he couldn't move.

The truck reached the Drive-In's parking area, bouncing over the gravel mounds and demolishing speaker poles in its path. Ranleigh watched as what seemed to be a shower of metal signs flew out from the truck's cargo bed, creating a surf-like rooster tail. The horse reared back in a frenzy, attempting to pull itself free from the speaker pole. Dallas Cooper lay motionless on the ground, making no effort to shield himself from the hooves raining down on his back, shattering his spine in three places. The truck surged forward with an unmistakable intent. It was a deliberate act.

The truck hit the horse with a sickening thud. The horse excreted a piercing squeal before collapsing. The truck came to a halt, and several minutes passed without any movement, leading Ranleigh to believe the horse was dead. Deep red streaks of blood stained the side of the truck.

From inside the truck, a voice erupted in a scream, "FUCK YOU! SEE IF YOU MAKE FUN OF ME AGAIN! SEE IF ANYONE MAKES FUN OF ME AGAIN!"

The shouting seemed to rouse the horse back to life. Its legs thrashed in an attempt to regain an upright position, while fragments of broken metal and horse flesh scattered in all directions. An awful grunt escaped, followed by silence. The truck reversed over the horse's legs and sped away across the prairie.

Ranleigh wasn't sure how long Coop had been bleeding from his mouth, obscured by the soot masking the blood. Coop's mouth moved as if he were trying to swallow or say something, but only clotted black stuff flowed out. Ranleigh recalled a fishing trip he had once taken with his father, the image of a fish gasping for air at the bottom of the boat clear in his mind. His father was drunk and laughing with the hint of violence looming, like the distant rumble of thunder, while Ranleigh begged him to throw it back over the side.

Uncertain of what to do, Ranleigh hesitated. He didn't want to leave Coop alone but knew things were really bad. The only thing he could think of was to hold Coop's hand. The cowboy's mouth opened and closed rapidly. Ranleigh thought again of his father and that fishing trip. Ranleigh couldn't find the right words to say to Coop, so he remained silent, squeezing his hand tight. Coop's grip weakened, and it was then that Ranleigh realized his friend was gone.

KINGLIN – Historic Landmark, Hewitt House, Ravaged by Suspicious Fire

By JOAN O'KEEFE

KINGLIN – In a devastating incident that unfolded just after 2:30 AM yesterday, Kinglin's renowned historic landmark, Hewitt House, fell victim to a raging fire of unknown origin. The inferno blazed uncontrollably for nearly two hours, leaving the roof and the interior of the house severely damaged. Tragically, Verna Hewitt, 68, the sole resident of the house, succumbed to smoke inhalation and was pronounced dead upon arrival at St. Peter's Hospital.

The first to discover the blaze was local rodeo legend Dallas Cooper, 52, who despite sustaining serious injuries earlier in the day while competing in the Kinglin Rodeo, made valiant attempts to rescue Ms. Hewitt. In an unfortunate turn of events, Mr. Cooper succumbed to his injuries early this morning a mile from the scene of the fire. The area has been cordoned off and the police are conducting an investigation.

Volunteer firemen Joseph Parsons and Sam Sanders, both from neighbouring Fairlawn City, were the first emergency responders at the scene, as confirmed by Fire Chief Fred Brown. Chief Brown stated that he and David Miller from the Provincial Fire Marshal's office will investigate the cause of the suspicious fire today.

In a bizarre postscript, Kinglin has fallen victim to a massive theft of street signs. A total of 44 signs, encompassing the entire town, vanished between midnight and 2 AM., according to police chief Tom White. Authorities are currently conducting a parallel investigation to determine if there is any connection between the stolen signs and the Hewitt House fire.

Four youths, all known to local authorities have been taken in for questioning.

Donald Webber and his wife, Ethel, residents of Kramden Ave, were peacefully asleep just a few houses away from the inferno when they were startled by the wailing siren shortly before 3 am "We looked out the window and saw the flames," recounted the Webbers. Eyewitness accounts, including theirs, reveal that the true hero of the night was 9-year-old Ranleigh Echo Meeks, residing on Main St., Kinglin. Holding onto the reins of an escaped stallion from the rodeo, young Ranleigh bravely led a group of 40 gathered residents in a rousing chorus of song to guide the firemen to the location of the Hewitt House. "Who knows?" pondered Ethel Webber. "Without the quick thinking of that little boy, the fire might have engulfed the neighbouring homes."

Once the volunteer firemen arrived, both Ranleigh Meeks and Dallas Cooper vanished from the scene. Following a brief but intensive search led by Chief White, Ranleigh Meeks was discovered early this morning a mile into the prairie, north of Kinglin, with the lifeless body of Dallas Cooper. Neither Ranleigh Meeks nor his grandmother was available for comment, as the young boy is currently under sedation at St. Peter's Hospital and is being treated for shock. He is expected to make a full recovery and is resting comfortably. Continued on page 3A

PART TWO

NIGHT OWL 1997

CHAPTER 13

Leigh Meeks jolted out of another dreamless sleep, immediately realizing he was still in the trap. Countless, dreamless nights of sleep and always back in the same trap. This waking realization had more to do with habit than conscious awareness. He automatically expected it. If he had been conscious of the thought, he would not have willingly chosen it because that would have been crazy.

This was not a thought arrived at by his reasoning mind. It was more like an electrical charge fritzing from someplace below. Deep below. Firing downward out of his head and through his body at the speed of thought and coming to an abrupt halt in his fingertips and toetips and waiting there patiently. Like the creature that lurks just below the surface of the murky water, only its yellow eyes visible, waiting to make its move.

His feet planted themselves on the floor before he knew what was happening. He had time for a shallow swallow of air and then that big, clear thought came: *Run.*

Leigh resisted the command as best he could but knew from experience that fighting it always made things worse. Fighting made everything worse. He recognized that playing out this pantomime dutifully, even if he couldn't do it entirely willingly, was the only option.

Struggling to his feet, Leigh grabbed for his cigarettes and lighter that sat on his bedside table, like the rotation of a carousel coming around to where your mother stands to give a big wave. He managed to catch the cigarettes and lighter then made his way down the hall, half running, half walking. Half walking, half running.

He experienced little variation in the routine from day to day. First, he checked the door. Somewhere along the line, Leigh had picked up a crippling fear of mail. Mail of any kind (even flyers). Added to this were delivery people, canvassers, and cookie-selling Girl Scouts, and because of this peculiar bent, he mostly avoided checking his mail slot whenever possible. It was, however, impossible to avoid any notices that might be slipped *under* the door.

When Leigh tried to analyze the fear, while riding on buses or walking in the local mall or sitting on park benches admiring water fountains, he would usually chalk it up to the irrational expectation of an eviction notice. Irrational because he knew he was all caught up with the rent. The other reason for the anxiety might be a letter informing him of work that needed to be done in his apartment or maybe just standard safety checks. Fire alarms and such. And indeed, that would mean *letting someone inside.*

Rationally Leigh understood that these things in and of themselves were not nearly enough reason to fuel the regular, morning shot of electric fear. What it felt like was more akin to finding a notice from the grim reaper himself tucked under the door, informing Leigh that his number was up and that on a certain, preordained date and time in the not-so-distant future, he would be annihilated from planet Earth in the most horrific of ways.

Something like this:

Dear Occupant,

We regret to inform you that come Friday, November 28, 1997, at 3:00

PM, we will need full access to your unit to complete the following work order:

we will lodge a food article deep in your throat (most likely a slippery string of bacon).

this will result in a sudden and complete elimination of any oxygen supply to your brain.

this will render any attempt on your part to call for help, useless.

you might claw at your throat in a state of desperate panic as we wrap up the work order.

upon completion of the work order, we will rip you from your human existence, while you beg for your life, suffering as much as is possible.

The work should be completed by roughly 3:15 PM.

Thank you,
-The Management

If Leigh were to describe the mental anguish he experienced every morning in the trap, something approximating this would be about halfway to the mark.

Moving down the hallway, eyes fixed forward, avoiding the bottom half of the door, Leigh would steel the few nerves left him and force himself to look down at the bottom of the door. Nothing would be there, of course. Next, the peephole. The fisheye lens gave him a partial view of the hallway. Normally all would be quiet, but he had to be sure, just in case. Struggling to turn the slippery deadbolt with sweaty fingers, Leigh would manage to get the door open, poke his head out and then peer left and then right. Nothing.

Usually, by this point in the routine, the electricity coursing through him would recede from a state of full panic to a lesser state of extreme anxiety. The benefit to this was that Leigh would find that the ability to think had returned. And the thought was always the same, one final stop on the panic train, and I will be able to light a smoke.

The kitchen table. A cheap, rotund table with far too many screws, designed in Sweden. Leigh could make it around the circumference of the table in seven paces, which he would commence doing after, and only after, he was quite sure that the hallway was safe.

"*Fuckfuckfuckfuckfuck*," Leigh would mumble to himself as he winged around the table. Around and around, he'd go.

"*Comeoncomeoncomeon*," he'd repeat, until finally the anxiety let go of him. In more reflective moments Leigh would think of this process as letting air out of a bursting tire.

In the end, Leigh would complete fifty full rotations, make his way to the living room couch, and collapse there. He would clock his heart rate at around 145 beats per minute, and although still in the trap, he would have regained partial control over his mind. And that was all he needed.

CHAPTER 14

The weather had taken a turn. It was cold. But the man sporting the bristly buzz cut was not. He was prepared. If nothing else in this miserable life, he was always prepared. An early-for-the-season snowstorm was on the way, barreling down on the unsuspecting residents of the city. The man felt an irritation rise in him as he peered out the window of the bus, wiping the condensation with his sleeve cuff in a windshield wiper pattern. Hopeless saps.

He could hardly believe how oblivious they were. Hadn't the storm been all over the news? And still, they drove around in their fancy cars without the minimum amount of foresight required to get their snow tires on. Hubcap after hubcap went by, with not a care in the world. Tempting fate. If the man owned a car, you could bet your last buck that he would have already been to the mechanic to have that taken care of. You betcha.

Hopeless saps.

The bus was crowded. The man had worked his way to the back and found a seat. He had briefly considered chatting with the driver but thought better of it. This driver was not one of his regulars. Not that he had anything against him personally (he was probably a decent, hard-working fellow), but clearly, he wasn't from *here*. He could always tell. He had a nose for this sort of thing. He figured the driver had probably come to Canada, intending to leech off the system, which would have been bad enough but to take a job, and a *good* job from one of the many out-of-work men who were at least born here, was intolerable to him. The man was certain he wasn't a racist, but goddammit, enough was enough.

What was so wrong about taking care of your own first, anyway? Just because they fucked up their own countries, didn't mean that they could come here and fuck ours up, too, he thought with fresh irritation.

Resting his forehead on the cool glass of the window, he told himself again that the security gig was only temporary. He didn't mind it too bad and besides, somebody had to watch the store, so why not him? Better him than some moron who would probably sleep most of the night away and let the labourers get away with murder.

The overnights were rough he had to admit, but it gave him time for other things. Working on his police application for one. The man had submitted a second application to the force and was sure he would get in this time. The last time he had applied, he had been too prideful. Too cocky. He knew that now. "If you were chocolate, you'd eat yourself," his mother would say to him. No more screwing around. This time everything was going to be different.

Cocky or not, he had always known that it was his destiny to be a police officer but knowing alone wasn't going to be enough. Back in high school, he had toyed with the idea of joining the armed forces, but in the end, he felt that being a police officer was the better fit. The seed that was planted first as a daydream matured into what the man now felt to be a *calling*, but clearly, he needed to pour some elbow grease on this vision, and he needed to get in shape if he expected to pass the physical.

"You're not fat, Jimmy," his mother would tell him while shoveling another heaping pile of Hamburger Helper onto his plate. "You're just solid. Built like my James was, God rest his soul."

The man had gone along with this logic his whole life, but when he began having a bit of trouble with the stairs while doing his security rounds, he was no longer so sure. Clutching his chest and gasping for air between the second and third floors wasn't caused by a solid build. And hadn't his father died of a heart attack?

He believed his mother loved him, but she didn't *understand* anything. And lately, the man had the traitorous feeling that she might not want him to succeed. That maybe she was sabotaging his efforts. Distracting him from his mission. Maybe she was afraid that he might leave for good. That he might finally strike out on his own and make something of his life. Wasn't it a little weird that she always seemed to need something from him when he was getting ready to go to the gym? Getting ready to go anywhere except work? Work was fine. Work brought in money.

At first, he couldn't see it because she was crafty. But hadn't she done the same thing to his father? If he was being honest with himself, wasn't that why he ultimately had his heart attack? And wasn't it too coincidental that she would always only have one of her spells just as he was packing his canvas duffel bag, the one he got cheap at the Army surplus store at Moss Park, to go to the gym?

"Jimmy! Jimmy, come here. Your mother isn't feeling too well. I'm feeling funny again, Jimmy. I think I might be in real trouble this time. Maybe you could sit with me for a while? I don't know what I'd do if something happened while you were gone. Maybe just stay here for a bit and when I'm back up on my feet, I will make you one of your favourites and we can watch the wrestling together. Huh, Jimmy?"

Earlier in the week the man had heard a couple of the female labourers talking in the lunchroom about something they called *boundaries* and for reasons beyond him, this got his full attention. This was not the usual, boring gossip, this was something different. He had pretended to take his time selecting something from the vending machine but was listening to every word they were saying.

These concepts were strange to him. Boundaries. Tough love.

What about loyalty? he thought to himself, pumping a shiny new toonie into the machine. *What about duty to one's only mother? What about all that honour thy parents' stuff? That was in the Bible!*

He was confused by this. Higher concepts like this took him some time for him. In school, they called him slow. He started grasping what they meant on the very outside edges with his fingertips but in no way could identify with it. Then out of the blue, somewhere between pressing the C and the 4 black cube-shaped buttons on the vending machine, it hit him. Hard. What registered was that this boundary thing might be his ticket out.

The bus was crowded. *Must be the storm*, Leigh thought. He was going to have to stand the whole way. He found it funny that crowds didn't bother him. Of his many anxiety problems, claustrophobia wasn't one of them.

"Meeks. Hey, Meeks!" The voice was coming from the back of the bus. Leigh could hear it over the music playing in his headphones, so the voice had to be loud. Leigh thought if he ignored it, the person might eventually give up. A logic as sound as a child who hides under a blanket in plain sight thinking no one can see her.

The woman standing beside him tapped his arm.

"I think the man back there is calling you," she said, looking annoyed.

Colonel Klink. Or at least that was what everybody at work called him behind his back, Leigh included. Jimmy was his name. Annoying for sure, but harmless.

"Hey, Meeks. Hey! Saved you a seat," Jimmy said, waving him over with one black-gloved hand, removing the duffle bag from the seat beside him with the other.

Jimmy had decided at some point that he and Leigh were friends with a capital F. This had become apparent to Leigh the previous Christmas when Jimmy had slipped him a Christmas card on the sly. Christmas cards were frowned upon in the workplace. Christmas trees and company Christmas parties would be next to go. They might turn a blind eye to the odd Happy Holidays or Season's Greetings card, but anything with baby Jesus or good old Santa Claus on the cover was strictly out.

And that Christmas when Leigh opened the envelope, he could see why. The card was creepy. And the fact that it appeared to be sincere made it all the more so. It read in large, gold cursive script, the name JESUS being prominent:
WORTHY ONE
EMMANUEL
GOD WITH US
THE WORD
JESUS
PRINCE OF PEACE
LIGHT OF THE WORLD
THE RISEN ONE
LORD
And inside, Jimmy's childlike printing:

Dear Leigh,
It looks to me like you might be the only other guy in here who even celabrates Christmas. We have to make sure that true believers like us stick together.
Have a Merry Christmas and may you find peace in the Lord this Christmas.
Youre friend,
Jimmy

Making his way to the back of the bus, Leigh was beginning to wish he had called in sick. If he had, he would not have run into the Colonel. And if he had not run into the Colonel, the Colonel would not have shown him the gun.

Leigh sat down beside Jimmy nearly breaking his ankle trying to step over the absurd duffle bag.

"Hey Jim," Leigh said.

"Oh, hey Leigh. Thought that might be you. What's up?"

Leigh shifted his weight over in his seat so that their thighs wouldn't touch. Ever since he was a kid, he hated the sensation of someone's thigh pressed against his.

"Yeah, sorry Jimmy. Couldn't hear you over the music," Leigh lied, tapping the earpiece with his index finger.

"I called a few times. Was wondering if you were ever going to hear me, or if I'd have to give your seat to somebody else," Jimmy said. An awkward silence followed.

"So, I see that you're still smoking, then?" Jimmy must have been watching him through the window while he waited to board the bus. "Those things'll kill you, you know. You should really think about giving them up. My aunt smoked like a chimney, and she died from it. Anyway, you should consider getting healthy, you know. Like me. I, myself am working on getting in shape. Going to the gym more. Got me a marine training program right out of Guns & Ammo. Seriously. The same one the guys in the Special Ops use. Maybe, I'd let you come along. We could meet up there before work and then ride in together. It's at Yonge and Bloor, right on the subway line. I heard somewhere that you're more likely to stick with something when you operate on what's called the buddy system," Jimmy said this all in one breath and leaned in a little too close on the word buddy.

Leigh shifted in his seat again.

"I'm personal friends with the guy who owns the gym, and I could probably get you a pretty good discount, you know, if you wanted to join."

"Sure, Jimmy. I'll think about it." Leigh lied.

"Really?" Jimmy said.

"Yeah, sure, Jimmy. Not making any promises, but I'll think about it," again, he lied.

During the next silence, Leigh calculated how much longer they had until their stop and figured it to be ten more excruciating minutes, give or take.

"Just coming from my community watch meeting," Jimmy said.

"Uh-huh," Leigh said.

"Yeah, I was able to get Mother's church to loan me the space for free. All it costs me is a box of doughnuts. Things started out pretty slow, but now I'm up to about seven members. I cover things like what to do if you see anything suspicious, how to defend yourself if you are attacked by a mugger, you know, that kind of thing."

Leigh almost laughed out loud at that one. He could practically see Jimmy putting a chokehold on some lonely old senior citizen who was there for the company and the free doughnuts.

Okay, now what do you do? Think fast, Grandpa!

"You can never be too careful these days, what with all the break-ins. I keep up with the stats," Jimmy said. "And that young offender's act is a disaster. Basically just giving permission to steal and get away with it."

"Yeah, I guess so," Leigh said.

As the bus slowed to a halt at the next stop, the only other person in their row got up and exited by the back doors and Jimmy seized the moment. Snow started falling.

Leigh felt a squirmy pressure the size of a meaty elbow digging in on his ribs. Everything about Jimmy irritated the shit out of him. Feeling the need to educate Jimmy on some home truths regarding the unspoken social contract of personal space, Leigh turned in his seat to see Jimmy motioning to the duffle bag with a not-so-subtle wagging of his chins.

"WHAT?" Leigh shouted over the din of the engine.

"Shut up, will you? What are you trying to do? Get me 'rested or something?" Jimmy said as he started rummaging around in the duffle bag.

"Listen, Jimmy. There's this thing called personal space. And elbowing me in the fucking ribs—"

It looked fake. It looked too black. It looked like it was made from heavy plastic. But, as usual, there seemed to be a wide divergence, Grand Canyon-wide, between what Leigh thought he knew and what he actually knew about certain things. The gun as it turned out, was real.

By the time all of this had settled in his head, Jimmy began elbowing him in the ribs for a second time.

"What the fuck, Jimmy?" Leigh whispered.

"Pretty cool, huh?" Jimmy seemed to transform right there in front of him, from an overweight security guard to a grinning child with a monumental secret. A secret whose seams are stretched to their capacity and ready to burst. A grinning child with a pistol.

"No, not cool, Jimmy," Leigh scolded him.

"What's your fucking problem, anyway? What's the big deal? Practically everybody has a gun these days," Jimmy said as he snapped the drawstring on the duffel bag shut. "And by the way, who died and made you King shit?"

Leigh turned away from Jimmy to look out the window at the falling snow. Time passed before Leigh spoke.

"What the hell do you need a gun for, anyway? And why bring it to work?"

"I told you already. What are ya, SLOW? You can never be too careful these days. You should hear the things I'm hearing in my community watch meetings. Don't you read the papers? And work? Work's no problem. I'm security. I'm the one who checks the bags coming in and going out, remember? I'm the top of the heap, my friend." Jimmy was trying to keep his voice down, but he was getting excited. Leigh had seen him this way before.

"Okay, Jimmy. Just keep it down," Leigh said.

After another long silence, Jimmy seemed to come back to himself.

"Don't you remember what happened last month?" Jimmy said, looking for another way to bring Leigh over to his side.

"Yeah, what about it?" Leigh said.

Leigh knew exactly what Jimmy was referring to. Leigh had wrapped up his shift and was standing in line waiting to have his bag checked before leaving the warehouse. This was Jimmy's line and Jimmy was *thorough*. Other than his hourly rounds, this was Jimmy's time in the spotlight. His time to shine. His reason for being. And he relished every minute of it.

That Wednesday morning after a mind-numbing overnight shift, Leigh could hear Jimmy and Saeed going at it. At first, Leigh didn't pay much attention, but things were getting heated. The line had gone silent.

Leigh didn't know Saeed. Maybe enough to say hello. He couldn't remember how he knew that Saeed was a father and had three kids at home, but he did know that. He couldn't imagine supporting a family on what they made at the warehouse, but Saeed seemed to be making a go of it and was usually in good humour. He also knew that Saeed had fought in a war back home in Afghanistan. Something to do with Russia. Leigh decided that Saeed was not someone he would want to antagonize, but Jimmy was a fucking idiot.

"What the fuck was that guy's problem, anyways?" Jimmy continued. "Not my fault I caught him with his hand in the cookie jar. The guy shouldn't a been stealing in the first place if you ask me. And why would he stick the DVDs right there in his bag where I would see them? Why wouldn't he at least try to stick a couple in his coat, or down his pants? Don't you see, he left me no choice!" Jimmy was getting excited again.

Jimmy had waved Leigh through that morning, as he and Saeed were getting into it at the security desk half hoping Leigh would stick around and back him up.

"Then what do you suppose these are then, my friend? I caught you red-handed. I'm going to have to write you up," Jimmy said, waving a couple of Disney DVDs in the air.

As Leigh passed by the security desk, Saeed slammed his hand down hard in front of Jimmy. The war scar on his face flushed bright red, it ran the length of his neck and up over his jawline like his skin had been scooped out with an iron-hot ice cream scooper. The sharp sound caused Jimmy to jump back, then he caught himself. He looked to Leigh with the old *aren't you going to help me out here?* look, but Leigh was already at the back door. Not wanting to be anywhere near Saeed when he went off, Leigh split.

"Don't know what you heard but turns out he was stealing kid's DVDs. You know, like the premium Disney titles. He actually tried to convince me that they were for his kids to watch and that he was planning on returning them. Ha! Nice try. For his kids, my ass. Everybody knows that you can get quite the pretty penny for those on the black market, especially those Disney movies. Anyway, he kicked up quite a fuss, but I held my ground," Jimmy said.

Leigh heard the next day that Saeed had been let go. The company opted not to press charges, but Saeed was gone. Leigh felt sorry for him and wondered what he was going to do with all those kids.

"Was pretty surprised myself, to tell you the truth. Would never have pegged Saeed as a thief and I'm usually pretty good at reading people that way. And that my friend is why I'm gonna make a great cop. It's mostly the black guys that do the stealing, though." Leigh winced. "Just goes to show you, you never know. And with a family and everything. A guy comes to our country, and you give him a chance and look what he does with it. Throws it away. Anyway, he was just lucky I kept my cool," Jimmy said.

It had become clear to Leigh why Jimmy felt he needed a gun. What would happen the next time Jimmy caught someone stealing? Or what if the next person he got fired came back for him? What if Saeed came back? Jimmy was scared. Jimmy was scared that next time might be tonight.

Leigh could barely contain his desire to get as far away from Jimmy as possible.

"Anyway, you haven't said much. Not going to turn me in for the gun thing, are you?" Jimmy said squinting. Testing the limits of an imaginary friendship.

"Nah, Jimmy. Your secret's safe with me," Leigh said.

"Thought so. Thanks, buddy. Not that I think he'd actually do anything, but Saeed fought in some fucking holy war or something. Maybe he'll come back, maybe he won't. But what he doesn't know is this, if he does, I'll be ready for him. Payback time. If only I was packing when I was in high school. Things would have turned out a lot different for me."

"I bet they would have," Leigh said.

81

Leigh and Jimmy exited the bus together. Lurching forward, Leigh vomited all over the snow.

CHAPTER 15

Four hours remained on the shift. The job was simple: the warehouse functioned as a fulfillment centre for retail stores in the province that sold DVDs, CDs, and books. Orders were processed during the day in the front office, requiring efficient packaging and readiness overnight for loading onto early morning trucks.

After Leigh punched his employee number into the new computer terminal, a cascade of SKU numbers would roll out of the printer. Curiously, they were never organized by category. Armed with his list, Leigh navigated through the towering rows of DVDs, CDs, CD-ROMs and books, the shelves stretching from floor to ceiling. Over time, he became a master, internalizing the labyrinthine of aisles and instinctively charting the fastest route to collect the designated items, which he boxed with grace. Leigh's proficiency, however, inadvertently drew unwanted attention from his coworkers. He completed three orders for every one they managed.

Months earlier, while deep in the recesses of one of the aisles, Leigh found himself cornered by Crystal, an older coworker. Crystal had parked her container and lit up a smoke, watching Leigh's frenzied ascent, then the descent of the mountainous, rolling safety ladder.

"Hey kid," Crystal interrupted, casually dropping her cigarette lighter into the pocket of her powder blue, regulation smock. Crystal looked to be a woman in her late sixties but was probably ten years younger. Her meticulously manicured nails seemed too long for packing boxes.

"Oh, hey. Crystal, right?" Leigh greeted her with a friendly smile.

"That's me, honey," she said tapping her name tag. "You catch on quick. Trying to set a new record here or something? Last I checked, there wasn't no Guinness Book of Records for the fastest box packer."

Leigh's smile widened, assuming Crystal was being friendly. "Just makes the night go a little faster, I guess."

Crystal leaned in closer, her voice lowered. "Yeah, well you're new and judging by the look of you, I can tell you're not in this for the long haul. Like a layover between flights, right? Never been on a plane myself. It just ain't natural," Crystal picked at the filter of her cigarette with an immaculate red thumbnail.

Leigh made his way down the ladder.

"Anyways, honey. Fallen on hard times? Lost all your trust money gambling in Vegas or just put it up your nose? Whatever. You need to fall in line. Because I am not going to have some Joe College getting me fired or put up for review because his orders are boxing up quicker than mine. I finally got a little seniority here. My hourly is up to the highest in the place and I'm finally able to get a little more vacation time to spend at my trailer next summer and I aim to keep it that way," she said, dropping her unfinished cigarette to the floor, making sure it was dead with a stomp of her steel-toed boot. "I don't need some hotshot jeopardizing that. Are we clear?"

"Crystal," Leigh said.

"Don't get smart with me, young man. Just keep your head down, blend in and we'll be fine," she said, dropping her lighter into a front pocket on her light blue smock.

From that point forward, Leigh slowed right down. And

because he listened, Crystal rewarded him with occasional nuggets of insider knowledge. The best spots on the warehouse floor to have a smoke and not get caught by the cameras and how to squeeze a little extra time out of the half-hour lunch break.

Despite the minor gains he had made by falling in line with Crystal's orders, the overall slowdown in his productivity was *excruciating*. It was as if he were working underwater, and he never got his rhythm back. He had succumbed. Leigh had officially joined the ranks. Filling the next box. And the next.

The amount was wrong. Short by a lot. Leigh never bothered much about whether the hours on his paycheck aligned with the time he sacrificed in that wretched place, but even he could tell this was way off. He had looked it over twice on the bus ride home and now, sitting in his kitchen, he furthered his investigation.

Ever since leaving high school, where the final flickers of hope had been extinguished for good, Leigh had toiled through countless jobs, each paying barely above the minimum wage. Some even less.

The warehouse stint was a slight improvement, but he still only received a paltry $8.85 for every hour of his life that he gave them, and the lunch hour wasn't included. He gave up more than half his earnings for the privilege of living in an area that, while not the worst in the city, came pretty close. Whatever money remained in his pocket was devoured by cigarettes, coffee, transit and food and the odd movie. He had to squirrel away money for work boots with steel toes when he moved from telemarketing to warehouse work.

When the paycheck went screwy, he didn't eat. When the money dipped far below the acceptable threshold, he didn't pay the rent. And in this instance, the amount was dangerously wrong. And although he felt a momentary swell of gratitude that his anxiety levels were holding, he was unable to hold the vomit that now dripped from the edge of the kitchen table and onto the floor.

Staring at the mess in front of him, Leigh glanced at his watch - it was already 8:30 AM. Ordinarily, he would have already eaten, but that was out. He needed a shower. Leigh decided he would deal with the vomit after some sleep, despite the smell. He had the impression that if he were to start the clean-up now, he might throw up again.

As he rinsed the remains of the vomit from his arms and hands in the shower, an image seized his mind. An amateurish, photocopied flyer advertising the merits of meditation. He had seen it pinned to the bulletin board of the public library, offering a free course on Thursday evenings. It was obvious to Leigh why, in this moment of stress, a thought like that would come to him and he was thankful for the fleeting diversion, although it did little to help with the odour.

Meditation, a goddamn mystery.

Leigh knew jack shit about it, just visions of Indian Holy men in loincloths he had seen on TV, sitting in the lotus position, chanting their cosmic OM. But he was hanging by a thread, anxiety buzzing around that puke-covered kitchen table like flies. Leigh figured he had nothing left to lose. No one to judge or mock him. So, right then and there, Swami Leigh decided to take the plunge.

Leigh started off trying to sit in what he thought might be a Zen-like position, legs crossed, on the floor by his bed. But his legs were beat from standing all night. So, he said fuck it and went against the grain. He opted for a prone position, head turned to the side. Lying flat on his chest, Leigh tried to relax. Easier said than done. His breath was shallow, nose stuffed up from breathing that dusty warehouse crud for the last eight hours. Like his body itself feared taking a full breath.

His jaw was clenched, then trembled when he tried to let it hang loose, so he closed it again which made it tremble more. His heart pounded on the mattress, loud as hell in his ears. No good. How the fuck was he supposed to meditate with all this body stuff going on? He almost gave up before even starting the OMing.

He took another deep breath and barely heard the trembling OM escape his lips, skipping like a stone on a calm lake. It sounded weird. Maybe Jimmy had a point, maybe he should quit those cigarettes. Jimmy. Prick. Deep breath. OM, he squeaked again, worse than before. Feet are freezing. Maybe get under the covers and start fresh? This isn't working at all. Stomach hurts.

By the time the third OM slipped out, his thoughts were running wild, his breath shallow and worrying, heart pounding worse than ever, jabbing pain in the left shoulder, but something deep inside spoke up. A voice that wasn't his own said, "Try counting."

This must be it, Leigh thought. This must be the point where sanity and I part ways for good.

But something inside him trusted that voice. So, without thinking too much, another laboured breath in, counting one, exhale. Breath in, two, exhale. Breath, three, exhale. Breath, four, exhale. By the time he hit twenty, breath and number blended. At seventy-six he felt like he was floating, separate from it all, breathing and counting going their own way. At ninety, he went higher still.

Leigh kept on counting, reaching two thousand that morning, but he couldn't tell you when he passed three hundred. Everything in his shitty world faded out. Leigh floated high above it all, till he folded into sleep.

And from that moment on, Leigh's life would never be the same.

PART THREE

MEEKS INHERITS THE EARTH

CHAPTER 16

Awake with eyes wide shut, he had awoken to the realm of space. Leigh floated, weightless and at peace, a figure adrift. The chains of anxiety had unraveled and retreated into the void. The waking fear that had haunted him always was no more and this was new for him. In this place, Leigh felt no distinction between the air in his lungs and the air that enveloped him. No longer caught in the twisting of separateness, he felt oneness with where he lay. The only lingering emotion was a mild worry that if he opened his eyes, he might break the spell. So, he basked in the internal sunshine a while longer.

The soft sheets and the pillows felt unfamiliar. The smell of fresh washing was in the air. This was not his bed, but no alarm came to him. Leigh was only experiencing, he was not attaching (not yet anyway). Absorbing the pillow's warmth, he wondered what time it was. To satisfy this curiosity, Leigh was willing to risk opening his eyes just a smidge. He had assumed the anxiety would crush him when he did but that was okay. Today he would be prepared.

A bedside clock, an antique artifact, sat on the table. It was not his. Silver bells crowned the face, its hands pointed to ancient Roman numerals. 9:39 AM or PM he wondered, for the room was dark.

If it's PM, I'll be late for work, Leigh thought, but he didn't care at all. He fixated on the clock's face, minutes ticking away like water dripping from a leaky faucet. How in God's name did that clock get there? Yet, it was the other objects on the night table that captured his attention. A cellular phone, a wad of cash, the sharp glint of silver on a money clip, sunglasses, a wallet, and a set of keys. An unsettling realization pierced through – this was not his bedroom, and this was not his bed, Daddy Bear. But the sense of familiarity surrounded him and persisted, like a child tugging on his pant leg.

This *was* his bedroom, and these were his artifacts – the clock and the keys.

Leigh reached for the money and counted it, and the sheer number of bills made his belly feel full. He opened the wallet, thumbing out credit cards and discarding them on the bedspread, his name embossed on the bottom corner of every one. Business cards were next with his name and his number. Then a revelation struck him. The keys were for the apartment he now occupied and for a car nestled in the parking garage. Key cards beckoned him to an unknown swimming pool and gym. How he knew all of this, he could not fathom.

The cellular phone rattled, jolting Leigh to attention. He was living fully in the moment now. Moments unfurled before him in peaceful succession – open your eyes, behold the clock, grab the cash, then the phone rings. Moment. Moment. Should he answer? He let it vibrate while blocking it from sliding off the edge of the night table with his palm.

Leigh drew himself up into a sitting position on the side of the bed, moving the bedspread to one side while draping the sheet over his lap. His body felt different, and he couldn't help but notice that moving had been easier and the persistent pain in his lower back was gone. The phone buzzed again, and again he decided to ignore it.

Leigh stood up, letting the covers fall from his lap. Casting aside any trepidation, he crossed the dark bedroom completely naked, flinging wide the door to the abyss that awaited him.

The expansive living room shrouded in darkness, revealed an otherworldly piano. As if guided by an unseen hand, Ranleigh walked directly to it and sat down. The music unfurled across the stand looked like computer data sheets covered in strange dots, but he knew he could play, though he had never taken a lesson in his life.

A solitary photograph encased in a silver frame stared back at him from the top of the piano. Time had aged the picture, a formal portrait from times gone by. An elderly woman, dressed for a forgotten occasion, her white hair making her appear much older than she was. Ranleigh recognized the woman instantly and felt the warm tears on his face. It had been a long time since he had seen her.

Grandma.

CHAPTER 17

10:01 AM. Leigh's hands were shaking too badly to light the cigarette. Fear flooded his senses, mixing the familiar metallic taste with his saliva as waves of electric shocks of physical anxiety surged through his arms. Despite completing the routine, his trips around the kitchen table had done little to alleviate the panic he was experiencing. He needed to get a hold of himself.

The dream had only made things worse, an unprecedented experience for someone unaccustomed to having dreams at all. This was one for the books. It unfolded like a bright, bold, technicolour, hallucinogenic, 3D acid trip. A feeling akin to a white-light-religious experience. Disoriented, he questioned what was real, if only momentarily upon awakening. An anxiety attack was the jolt that jarred him back to reality. If it had not been for the familiarity of the *trap*, he might never have come back to himself.

Leigh knew next to nothing about dreams. Of course, he had heard, like every kid had, that if you die in your dream you fall into a coma in real life, but he dismissed those stories as urban myths and dream interpretation as a load of bullshit.

However, during his high school years, the concept of lucid dreaming captured his imagination. This was the dream that everyone wanted to have, (and some claimed to be able to do, of course, more bullshit). The idea was that you could have a dream that unfolded in real time. You would walk through the dream minute by minute, and it would be so real that it would appear to you as if you were living in an entirely different reality, a reality of your own making. Of course, the most appealing part of that to any high school kid: was, *you could do whatever you wanted.*

Seated on the couch, staring at the unlit cigarette perched on the coffee table's edge, Leigh wondered what the greater burden was. Was it better to have had the experience of the lucid dream and pay for it with the extra helping of panic the dream seemed to heap on him this morning when he woke up or to not have had the dream at all? Given the choice, he would still take the dream.

Another astonishing realization surfaced – a long-forgotten dream from his childhood returned with vivid clarity. He must have been nine or ten and what felt this morning like the first dream he ever had, turned out to be the second. Memories flooded back as he stared out of the cramped apartment window that morning, half expecting the arrival of police cars that never seemed to arrive, he remembered everything. The imagined presence of a grandmother he never had, the tragic rodeo accident involving Dallas Cooper that never happened, the haunting image of Verna Hewitt being put into the body bag after a fire that never burned. Hell, Leigh had never even been to the prairies. He remembered it all and none of it was real.

CHAPTER 18

The office-side reception area of the warehouse building looked and smelled like a run-down motel lobby. Leigh had stayed in enough of those as a child to last him a lifetime. A flimsy wooden partition boldly showcased the company name at knee level, PackUcan. Positioned deliberately, the partition obstructed the view of the receptionist, forcing visitors to lean over the desk to get her attention.

PackUcan, owned by a multinational conglomerate headquartered overseas, seemed completely indifferent to the naming of its subsidiaries. Their marketing approach leaned more to direct translation rather than a localized creative branding approach. In addition to the ludicrous company name, the Canadian branch cared little for a timely and accurate payroll or ensuring common safety practices were followed, let alone fostering any kind of career growth.

What the company did care about were *name badges.* Curiously, their obsession lay in enforcing and wearing name badges. As far as Leigh understood it, every company employee overseas was required to wear a name tag, minus the standard *Hello my name is* salutation. Leigh had difficulty wrapping his head around it. While it made sense for public-facing employees in local Canadian fast-food joints or retail outlets to display their first names only, just to give that oh-so-personal touch, PackUcan took it to a whole new level. Regardless of position, all employees were required to wear a name badge featuring their first *and* last names above the company logo.

The enforcement of this policy fell to a peculiar individual. Unfortunately for Leigh, the person in charge of payroll was also the badge cop. Leigh had first laid eyes on her during tax season, her usual laziness replaced by a foul temper due to the added workload and late nights. To let off a little steam, armed with a notebook and pen, she prowled the aisles, gleefully noting any transgressors of the badge code.

Leigh mostly kept his badge tucked away in his pocket, attempting to get it on at the last possible moment upon hearing the click clack click clack of high heels echoing through the warehouse. However, he did not always make it, and he frequently fell victim to her watchful eye while sitting in the lunchroom, distracted by the music playing in his headphones. She would lurk behind the vending machine, observing him with a disapproving shake of her head, before recording his non-compliance in her notebook. Oddly, she never said a word, she would scribble down his name and walk away, but her peculiar enjoyment in the task was unmistakable.

Leigh couldn't abide by the security concerns related to the badge policy. He remembered reading about a tragic incident overseas involving a server at a relatively posh downtown restaurant (the restaurant in question also practicing the same bizarre name badge policy). This server had unwittingly managed to get herself on the radar of a timid, nice but mostly-kept-to-himself, yet menacing stalker who traced her back to her small apartment and after his many advances were politely rebuffed, gained entry through an unlocked window and ended her life by strangling her with her stockings. She was later found dead behind her apartment building in a dumpster and yes, she was still wearing the name badge, expediting the identification process considerably.

This concept of enforced identification poked a particular

nerve of Leigh's, pricking at his deeply engrained aversion to authoritarian tactics employed by mediocre managers in mediocre companies. Leigh felt such practices aimed to degrade employees, making it easier to push them around. While his coworkers mostly complied without question, Leigh resisted. He had gone as far as attempting a grass-roots uprising, only to be met with, "Sorry man, I can't afford to lose this job," or "Fuck off, Meeks."

Only Jimmy and the slightly terrifying Ron were the slightest bit behind him. Ron, standing six foot eight, whom Leigh would see occasionally lumbering around in grubby overalls would say, "Sure Leigh. Why don't you let me know how you make out? Need me to sign a petition or something?" Assigned to break down excess cardboard from DVD, CD, CD-ROM and book deliveries, Ron worked nine-hour overnight shifts mostly by himself and always wearing his name badge. At heart, Ron was a company man.

The lobby today was quiet, the receptionist hidden behind the partition, engrossed in a romance paperback. Leigh imagined her silently mouthing the words as she read. Despite being told to wait, Leigh knew Blaireau would see him, even without an appointment. Blaireau rarely passed up a chance to belittle an employee from the warehouse, despite how busy she pretended to be. The tension between the front and back was fueled by resentment, as encounters such as these always involved disgruntled workers making complaints.

"Ms.Blaireau will see you now," the receptionist announced.

Leigh half expected her to escort him to Blaireau's office, but she did not. He was required to sign himself in, name, date, time in, and contact at PackUcan. He would be required to sign out when the meeting was done. The receptionist also requested some identification, as Leigh wasn't wearing his name badge.

Leigh knocked on the open door. Blaireau raised a pudgy

finger, indicating she was busy and he would have to wait. Leigh observed her, focused on a computer terminal that was too small for the side table. Above her, a framed poster depicted a man conquering some mountain peak, with the words MAKE IT HAPPEN printed below. Blaireau hunched forward, engrossed in a spreadsheet glowing on the screen, her painted nail rhythmically tapping the glass. Eventually, with a flourish, she lowered her finger and clicked the obedient mouse, positioned to the left of the keyboard. Click.

While waiting, Leigh had time to take in all that was Blaireau. She was overweight but not yet obese (that would come later). She resembled the term pear-shaped in a literal way. Her self-dyed blonde hair featured silver frosting on the tips, a do-it-yourself job, as her pay would only allow infrequent visits to the salon.

Leigh couldn't help but view her pretentious air as a caricature of hopeless, middle management. Her business suit reminded him of a child dressing up and playing office, and this only amplified his impression. Leigh always felt most comfortable with people at the top or bottom of the ladder. He found little connection with those permanently stuck in the middle. The main problem with that was the people in the middle sometimes had enough power to inflict harm if you found yourself at the bottom. To eat, Leigh would have to play the game.

"Mr. Meeks. Please come in," she said standing, pointing to a chair in front of her desk. As she sat down the chair legs squeaked.

"Isn't it a little early for you? I thought you were on nights?" she huffed.

"Yes, I am. Uh, still am. Yes," Leigh said.

"So then, what can I do for you? And make it fast, I'm a busy woman. Lots to prepare for the big visit."

"Big visit?"

"Indeed, Mr. Meeks. Our owners are sending a delegation to Canada for a series of meetings, you might think of it as a road trip, and they are planning to visit our office last before heading home. It's a great honour for us."

"Sure, that's great. Let me know if there's anything I can do to help out," Leigh offered.

Blaireau scoffed openly, "I can assure you they won't be visiting the back of the store or during the middle of the night. Just do the job you're paid for. That should be sufficient."

Leigh's palms grew sweaty, and he felt his nails digging into his skin. "Right. Okay then," he said, shifting uncomfortably in his seat. His anxiety about the money was dissolving in a boiling stew of hatred.

"So, Mr. Meeks, I'll ask again, to what do I owe the pleasure of this unexpected visit?" Blaireau said.

"There's a problem with my last pay," Leigh said.

"Let me guess, it's less than what you expected," Blaireau said. "You people never come here complaining when it's more, do you?"

"Yes, it's less, quite a lot. Hoping we can resolve this today. I need that money," Leigh replied, his voice almost a whisper.

His face turned a combination of red, grey, and silver like the colour of dry, raging fuel rods in a nuclear reactor. A Rage that is the offspring of powerlessness and humiliation.

Blaireau raised a finger to silence him, then swiveled back to her computer. She slouched forward, clicking the mouse and typing with exaggerated noise, until she found what she was looking for.

"Here it is. Yes, I thought so," she said, her eyes still fixed on the screen. "You, my friend, are up to date and paid in full." Leigh's stomach lurched.

"That can't be right. I worked a full two weeks, and my pay was short by a whole week." Leigh was now fumbling with the envelope he had scribbled his calculations on as if it would strengthen his case. "And I know I didn't call in sick," Leigh added.

"No. No, you didn't," Blaireau replied, barely containing her satisfaction, still not looking away from the computer.

"I took all of my breaks on time and didn't go over. Not once."

"Correct."

"I punched in and out myself. I didn't skip out on a single shift," Leigh said, a confused desperation creeping over him. He was starting to realize that he would not be receiving the money at all, let alone into his bank account that afternoon.

"Please, check the security footage. I was there," he pleaded.

"Oh, I know you were there. I had Jimmy review the tapes for me."

"So, what then?"

Blaireau swiveled back, relishing the moment, allowing a grin to spread across her face like oil on water. "Name badge," she said.

The lunchroom was quiet as Leigh sat there, absentmindedly picking at a small scab on his left hand. The lingering itch of a cold burn beneath his skin was subsiding. Spending too much time in the cold had him wondering if there was any permanent damage to his hands. Sitting in the lunchroom made him hungry, but he had no food. He glanced up at the hooded security camera, flicked the name badge he now wore, and waved.

During his break, Leigh spent most of the time trying to work out how he was going to pay his rent. He had often wondered what would happen if he pushed the badge thing too far, now he knew.

He had completely ignored the yellow form letter tucked behind his paycheck. If he had bothered to read it, he would have discovered that he had been reprimanded four times in the past two weeks for not wearing official workplace attire. Warning notices had been placed behind his previous paycheck. Four infractions, resulting in a full day's wage deduction each, accounted for the missing money. Leigh attempted to question the legality of such severe consequences, but he was reminded of the documents he had signed during his hiring process, which included penalties for failing to display the PackUcan name badge prominently on the left side of his chest. Leigh was starting to realize that he should probably pay more attention to official documents. The agreement also stated that continued insubordination could lead to termination without notice or severance. Blaireau had actually tossed the document across the desk at him.

Infinite punishment for finite transgressions.

The rest of the evening was spent working out how he would make up for the shortfall, but the bleak reality was that he had no means to do so. Leigh Meeks was a person of little consequence. He didn't fit into any meaningful statistical chart. Unmarried, childless, minimal tax obligations, no university education, and even lacking in any statistically significant diseases. He never voted. Hell, he rarely ventured outside during daylight hours. The only positive thing you could say about Leigh's existence was his ability to scrape by and keep his head above water. Other than that, he was a rounding error, destined to be recorded as born and eventually marked as deceased.

Leigh had excused himself from Blaireau's office, traversed the lobby, and stepped onto the street. His shift wasn't scheduled to begin until 10 PM, and the meeting with Blaireau had finished at 4:30 PM, leaving him with time to kill. Unable to afford the bus fare to his apartment and back, he decided he would walk around. The thought of quitting crossed his mind, but he knew he wouldn't go through with it.

Leigh trudged through snow that was souring to slush, wondering why he hadn't succumbed to clinical depression yet. By the three-hour mark, he could no longer feel his feet. He was exhausted and his dwindling cigarette count only added to his misery. After four hours, he found himself back where he had started, having completed a full loop through the frozen industrial wasteland he had only ever observed from a bus window. *I'm literally walking in circles now*, he thought. *This must be what homelessness feels like.* The aroma of burgers and French fries wafted through the crisp air as he stood in front of a Burger King on the corner.

Returning to work after his ordeal, Leigh punched in and kept to himself, ensuring his name badge was securely fastened to his shirt. He knew Blaireau would inquire about it, hoping to see a display of courage he had failed so miserably to exhibit during their meeting. But as much as he yearned to shove that laminated square of corporate fire branding down her throat, he was powerless and compelled to comply. He was too exhausted to fight the system, too tired to do anything but set the alarm on his watch and rest his head on the lunchroom table.

Please, God, let me hear my alarm, I can't be late, he prayed silently.

CHAPTER 19

2:10 AM. "Ranleigh! Ranleigh, wake up. You're dreaming," the voice said. The room was dark. "Ranleigh?"

"Yeah, I'm awake," he murmured, his voice barely audible. "What time is it?" Ranleigh held the cellular phone up to his ear.

There was a pause on the line while the voice checked the time.

"Just after two," the voice said. "Try to go back to sleep," the tone carried an understanding that seemed unusual for the late hour. It was a woman's voice, the kind of voice that would stay awake with him until morning if that was what he needed.

"How many times did I try you? Was I screaming?" Ranleigh recalled his tendency to scream in his sleep during childhood. His mother would demand to know the content of his dreams, but he could never remember. She thought he was lying.

"No, you weren't screaming. You were talking, although it didn't make much sense. You sounded groggy, so I assumed you called me in your sleep. I think you might have been dreaming about money problems. Are you facing money issues? I could help. I could make them go away."

"What did I say?" Ranleigh's curiosity was piqued, though

lacking in concern. It was difficult to be concerned here.

"You said something along the lines of, 'There won't be enough. There won't be enough to eat.' Then you kept on repeating it, 'won't be enough, won't be enough.' I suppose that's when you came around."

He knew who she was. Her name was Charlotte, and she was his coworker, and he trusted her.

"Are you all right? Is there anything you want to talk about?"

Ranleigh felt himself drifting back towards the verge of sleep.

"No, Charlotte. I'm good. Like you said, probably just a bad dream. I apologize for waking you. Thank you for taking my call so late."

"That's all right, Ranleigh. Try to get back to sleep," she said.

Ranleigh didn't respond. Ending the call, he fought the urge to slip back into sleep. He wanted to stay here, but he succumbed to the pull of slumber.

Ron the cardboard man tugged on Leigh's arm, seated beside him at the lunchroom table.

"You were screaming. The others were getting scared. Sorry to wake you."

"Thanks," Leigh said.

"That must have been some dream," Ron remarked.

Leigh raised his head, rubbing the exhaustion from his eyes, attempting to focus on Ron.

"How long was I out?" Leigh asked, in a demanding tone. He needed the answer as quickly as possible, fearing he might have overslept. Ron was slow to respond. "What time is it?" Leigh added.

"It's two ten," Ron replied. "You're good, you got about fifteen more minutes."

"Thanks," Leigh said, wiping drool from the corner of his mouth.

"Better be careful not to let Crystal catch you sleeping like that during break time. She might write you up."

"Fuck her," Leigh muttered under his breath. "They already docked me two hundred and fifty bucks this pay."

Ron remained silent, shaking his head, and using the table for support, he stretched his six-foot-eight frame as he stood up. As Ron walked back to the recycling bay, Leigh called out after him.

"Hey, Ron. Thanks, man. You really saved my ass."

Without turning around, Ron replied, "I know the worry when you think there won't be enough. My mother used to tell me that kind of worry will put cancer in your belly."

As Ron disappeared around the corner, his words echoed faintly, "There won't be enough. There won't be enough." And then he was gone. It sounded like singing.

CHAPTER 20

In the weeks that followed, Leigh's life underwent a complete transformation and also remained entirely the same. Understanding the nature of his dreams was a gradual process and the first revelation was this: Leigh could now remember his dreams. The significance of this held him up for a day or two as it was a shock to Leigh that he could remember his dreams at all. This ability was both a gift and a disorienting experience.

Spending countless sleeping hours in darkness had taken its toll on Leigh. He had read somewhere that dreams operated like a central processor, helping to process information, resolve conflicting emotions, and make sense of nonsensical events. Leigh had long suspected that lacking this essential function made his waking hours more challenging to navigate and might actually be the cause of his morning anxiety problem.

His ability to dream now unfolded in real-time, giving him the sensory experience of never sleeping. Closing his eyes in one place, he would suddenly find himself sliding down a rabbit hole and awakening elsewhere, feeling refreshed. Initially, Leigh tried to understand the reasons behind this change in his sleep. He wondered if it was caused by the perpetual night shift. Of course, he was under immense pressure, not eating properly, smoking too much, and likely exposed to chemicals in the packaging warehouse (the boxes smelled like a combination of bleach and old cheese).

During the initial weeks, it would be inaccurate to assume that the dreams took centre stage in his life. They did not. Although he could recall his dreams upon waking up, they slipped away as reality took hold, and his anxiety routine would start up again.

Over those first few weeks, Leigh struggled to make ends meet. He would search behind couch cushions and check the pockets of long-forgotten summer clothes piled up in his closet, hoping to find enough change to buy cigarettes. When desperation struck, he would rummage through the same pockets a second and third time. He was living hand to mouth and the hand was coming up empty. To save money, he started walking to work instead of taking the bus (walking home after a long shift was not an option). He survived on pasta, rationing the tomato sauce. He drank tap water and limited his coffee consumption to the minimum amount required to stave off the blinding headaches and nausea caused by caffeine withdrawal. Despite these sacrifices, he still wasn't sure he'd make the rent.

In those first few weeks, Leigh was preoccupied by the precariousness of his situation. Perhaps because of malnutrition or the tremendous physical exertion from walking to work in the snow and spending eight hours on his feet, he failed to notice the most obvious aspect of his dreams. Although he could see clearly that the dreams appeared repetitive in those first few days, he missed something more mystical and frightening.

The dreams were progressing sequentially.

In learning that his dreams were mirroring the passage of time in his waking life, he became much more interested in what the next dream would bring and far less interested in his daily life. Leigh started looking forward to returning home in the morning after finishing his night shift, switching off the bedroom light, and diving straight into bed, hoping the dream would not pick up where it had left off, but instead aligning with the time he fell asleep in his cramped apartment.

Skipping breakfast after a long night was easy since there was nothing in the fridge to eat. In recent days, he had foregone brushing his teeth or taking off his clothes. He would simply open the front door, kick off his wet boots, and crawl into an unmade bed. As he drifted off, he would silently pray, addressing no one in particular, please let the dreams continue.

Leaving his dreams behind and abruptly crashing back to so-called real life became increasingly difficult. The morning anxiety ritual still plagued him, albeit with less ferocity and duration compared to a few weeks earlier. As he predicted, he couldn't afford to pay his rent in full, which ignited a new and significant spark of fear. Leigh had been careful to wear his name badge, fand or Jesus' sake, making sure he didn't lose it. Instead of writing a cheque for a partial amount and risking a confrontation with the landlord, he decided to hold back the entire payment until he was ready and able to pay in full. In other words, the cheque was in the mail.

One evening while rummaging through the back of his kitchen drawers before leaving for work, Leigh stumbled upon a stack of envelopes and a few stamps. It had been years since he'd written a letter to anyone, but that evening a strong impulse compelled him to put pen to paper if only to document the dream phenomenon he had uncovered.

It's been ages since I wrote to anyone, so you should consider yourself lucky. I used to have a pen pal when I was a kid, I think, remember those? Pen pals. But since then I haven't felt like my life was worth writing about. And besides, who would I tell? You, I suppose. Since these dreams started happening, I thought it might be worth putting them into words. But honestly, I don't expect the dreams to stick around.

These dreams began a couple of weeks ago, around the same time my anxiety started getting the better of me. I wondered if there might be a connection, but I'm still not sure.

The fact that I've never dreamed before has made this experience even more intense. Let me try to describe it. I have no clue where these dreams come from or what they even mean.

First, these dreams feel completely real to me. I have no idea if other people's dreams are this vivid. Are yours?

Secondly, the dreams play out in real-time. What I mean is that when I get home from my graveyard shift at the warehouse around 6:45 AM and fall asleep at 7:30 AM, the dream starts up right at 7:30 AM on the same morning. It took me a day or two to figure that out initially.

I always 'wake up' in the same bed, in the same room, but the dream itself is never the same. More on this later. Then I go through the entire day minute by minute, just like I do when I'm awake. I've read that dreams usually jump around and mess with the dreamer's sense of time, but that hasn't happened to me, not once.

The dream lasts as long as I sleep, but in these real-time dreams, that takes on a different meaning. Are you confused yet?

When I wake up from the dream in the evening to get ready for my night shift at the warehouse, the dream ends, and I fall back into reality. So, my dream day lasts from around 7:30 AM until about 3 PM.

Now here's the third thing I figured out, though it took me a couple of weeks. The dreams are sequential, and as far as I can tell they all take place here in Toronto, in the current year, month and day. At first, I thought it was just a repetitive dream, like that movie Groundhog Day a few years back. But then I dozed off in the lunchroom one day around two in the morning and woke up in my dream life at 2 AM, right in the middle of a phone conversation. Later that week I looked at my wall calendar and realized what was going on. So, these dreams have been following each day, just like my real life does. But here's the strange part: my real life and dream life couldn't be more different.

Lastly, in these dreams, I have full control. It's not like I'm being pushed along on some autopilot. I have what I can only describe as free will. I think I recognize the dreams as dreams when I am in them, but I'm not entirely sure yet. I have freedom of choice and I am still me. I can't fly or have any superpowers. I can't read minds or turn invisible. I don't feel the urge to rob a bank.

I'm still not sure if there are consequences in the dream place, but I assume it operates much like reality does. And although I'm still me at heart, I feel different from the person I am here. Everything about me is different. It's like I've been built or moulded from a different set of experiences, and when I enter this dream state, this place, I somehow know that. It's hard to explain. For example, in the place, I now know I'm a successful writer. I don't have any memory of writing novels there, I just know I have done it. It's more like a deep knowing than a remembering.

There, I am successful. Here, I am not. I can feel that difference. It's like I'm running from a different originating program. I feel confident there, but when I come back, all of that confidence vanishes. Obviously, I can remember what happens there, which allows me to write it down, but it doesn't translate to the real world. I can't be that person here.

There I have ongoing conversations with a woman who works with me, although we've never met. It took a while to figure out, but she's my literary agent, Charlotte, and she lives in New York City. We talk on the phone regularly and have planned to meet up for dinner, but I am not able to make it to dinner time in my dream.

As much as I want to meet her in person, I still have to work at the warehouse and can't afford to call in sick, so sleeping longer is out of the question. I'm late on my rent, too. Just to be clear, I am not asking you for anything. This isn't some elaborate scheme.

One thing I noticed right away is how I feel in the dream place. You know about my lifelong struggle with anxiety. It's always there, some level of fear and worry. When I wake up it's the worst and lately, it's been edging down a bit. But in the place, fear doesn't exist at all. I can't stress how monumentally fucking huge that is for me. From the very first dream, it felt like I could actually breathe. I felt surefooted and confident.

In my real life, I am constantly battling fear, and it's been holding me back. It's hard to explain to someone who hasn't lived with this curse like you haven't. But imagine going through your day with a constant hum of fear vibrating through your body, and an ever-present sense of dread following you like a dark cloud. You're talking to someone, like a bank teller or the cardboard recycling guy or a security guard and suddenly your mind screams at you, GET OUT! IT'S NOT SAFE! Your rational mind tells you everything is fine and normal, that your friendly co-worker couldn't possibly be reaching for the shotgun he stole from his dad that morning right before blowing his head off. And yet, you stay, politely wishing them a good night, praying like hell you'll make it out of there alive. That's how the fear feels.

And that's just on a good day. That's a manageable day. But in the place, all of that is gone. I've been released from it. Saved, maybe. Here, I'm disappointed most of the time.

Navigating the city in the dream is no problem because it's all happening here in Toronto. I live in the Colonnade building on Bloor Street. I've never been in that building, but in the dream, I know what's around every corner. In the basement parking garage, I own a car. Here, I've never owned one. I spent days just cruising around the city at first.

Meeting my agent Charlotte in person is becoming an obsession. If the dreams continue, I'll have to figure out a way to make it happen.

I hope everything is well with you.

Love,
Leigh

CHAPTER 21

The Colonnade on Bloor looms over the smaller boutiques that cater to Toronto's deep-pocketed patrons. Stores like Versace, Cartier, and Tiffany's that line Toronto's mink mile appear to be building block foundations that supported the Colonnade's massive structure and perhaps they are. Ranleigh Meeks had never stepped inside the Colonnade itself, but in his teenage years, he would occasionally pass by after taking in a movie at the enormous University Theatre, demolished in 1986, across the street.

In those initial days, it came as a shock to find himself in one of the penthouse apartments, complete with a private garden, an outdoor patio offering panoramic views of Lake Ontario to the south and Rosedale to the north, and a private swimming pool. At first, Ranleigh didn't even realize that he was in the Colonnade – it was only when he ventured outside that he recognized it.

The apartment was beautifully decorated, a testament to the considerable amount of money spent with no expense spared. Ranleigh had found the expansive living room on that first morning, dominated by a large, buttery leather Chesterfield and matching loveseat. A baby grand piano and a large flatscreen (new to the market in 1997) were positioned on the other side of the room. Although Ranleigh couldn't recall purchasing any of these items, he knew that he had approved the purchase through a decorator named Judy.

A second bedroom served as an office, minimalist in its décor, with a massive wooden desk positioned in the centre of the room, facing away from the picture windows. To the immediate left of the desk stood a glass cabinet, illuminated from the inside, housing what appeared to be numerous awards. Directly facing the desk, on the opposing wall, a colossal bookcase squatted and stretched from floor to ceiling, filled with every book he had ever heard of, all of which he knew he had read.

Ranleigh was run down from working nights, so to be in this sanctuary was a blessing. He spent his first days in the place watching the flatscreen television, reading the books he himself had written, and generally taking it easy, being mindful not to fall asleep. That was the cardinal rule. He could do what he liked, as long as he didn't fall asleep.

He marvelled at the quality of the books he had written. One series, classified as fiction but largely based on truth, centred on organized crime. The second book had been adapted into a film and won him a Genie Award for best-adapted screenplay. The award was presented to him by Bruno Gerussi.

Ranleigh knew that most of the research for the book series came from a friend of his named Massimo, who owned a neighbouring restaurant in Yorkville, Massimo's on Bay. Massimo had been involved in organized crime in Quebec, before moving to Toronto in 1979 to open the restaurant. Whenever Ranleigh needed a fact check or more colour for a manuscript, he and Max would meet for dinner and talk into the night. Max was more than happy to set him straight on all that water under the bridge, giving the stories a shape that would have otherwise been absent.

After those first few days of hanging around the apartment, Ranleigh felt ready to venture out. Awakening in the dream place at exactly 8:04 AM, he enjoyed a substantial breakfast from a fully stocked fridge and coffee before leaving through the front door and heading to the elevator. No *fuckfuckfuck*. No circles around the kitchen table.

The lobby bustled with people on their way to work, and Ranleigh maneuvered his way through the crowd, making his way out onto Bloor Street. It was then that he realized where he was in the city. It took a minute to get his bearings, but when he turned back to look at the towering concrete structure, he instantly recognized it.

Ranleigh lifted his gaze toward the penthouse, feeling his good fortune when someone tugged at the sleeve of his jacket. Startled, he reflexively thought, *this must be it. I've been found out. I've been caught.*

Turning toward the coat tugger, half expecting to see Jimmy standing there, Ranleigh felt relieved to find himself face-to-face with a stranger. The man appeared to be in his early fifties, with a full white beard and thinning salt and pepper hair. He was fashionably dressed and wore red-framed glasses. Handsome enough, but Ranleigh thought he would have been more attractive in his youth.

"Excuse me," the man said.

"Do I know you?" Ranleigh replied.

"I'm afraid not," the man said. "Forgive me. I saw you come out of that building and felt compelled to approach you. You see, I have read everything you've written and I'm a huge fan. I just wanted to tell you what your work means to me and perhaps shake your hand."

Ranleigh took a moment to adjust to the pantomime, then shook the man's hand vigorously. He thanked him for the compliment, and the man requested an autograph, to which Ranleigh readily agreed. This scene would repeat itself several times throughout the day. It did not become annoying or tiresome.

After strolling along Bloor Street, a small coffee in his hand, Ranleigh decided on the Versace store on the south side. He was well aware, like anyone with access to TV, radio or newspapers, that Gianni Versace, the renowned fashion designer had been shot in the head by a man wearing black shorts and a white hat on the front steps of this mansion in Miami Beach, Florida.

Upon hearing the news one evening before his shift at PackUcan, Ranleigh felt compelled to purchase something designed by the murdered fashion icon. Of course, he couldn't afford to buy anything there, let alone justify a needless trip downtown on the subway, but he felt he should just the same.

In the dream place that day, he bought a Versace tie and scarf. He kept the tie in the black paper bag with the black tissue paper, while he wrapped the scarf around his neck.

By one o'clock, hunger struck Ranleigh. Carrying shopping bags from Gucci, Hazelton Lanes, and Hugo Boss, he made his way down Cumberland Street. Taking a sharp right turn up Old York Lane, he paused to admire a mural depicting the lane as it appeared in 1852. It depicted a house with a series of four windows—one partially obscured by an autumn-stained tree, another displaying a couple locked in an embrace, a third displaying a sign advertising violin lessons, and in the fourth, a glass bottle of milk cooling on the sill.

A hand-painted caption read, "*You are standing on Old York Lane, in the heart of the village of Yorkville. Incorporated in 1852, the village was later annexed to the City of Toronto in 1883. Enjoy.*" The lane itself was lined with specialty shops on one side, small billboards lined the other, advertising sunglasses, watches, and condominiums.

Remy's restaurant was located at the north end of Old York Lane. Ranleigh swung open the doors, climbed the two steps leading to the bar, and dropped his bags at his feet before taking a seat. The restaurant was empty, except for an older, well-dressed man who looked to Ranleigh like a frog in a silk suit and a biker with the reddest hair Ranleigh had ever seen, sitting at the end of the bar. Seated by a window adjacent to the lane, across from the frog sat a much younger woman in a little black dress, her hair pulled back too severely for her age. The bartender, a middle-aged blonde woman, took Ranleigh's order, then resumed her conversation with a biker at the end of the bar.

After half a glass of red wine, Ranleigh approached the bartender and asked where the washroom was. She directed him to a narrow stairway behind the bar and offered to store his bags behind the counter until he returned. The staircase smelled of spilled alcohol and cigarettes.

Ascending the stairs, the door at the top revealed a room of comparable size to the one below, with all the charm of a basement in a frat house. Two worn-out leather sofas, a deserted bar stacked high with cardboard boxes, and a dilapidated pool table with faded purple felt occupied the space. Ranleigh walked past the pool table, pausing momentarily to roll the white ball into one of the corner pockets. Just as he did, he heard the sound of a flushing toilet from behind a door that read MEN.

The washroom was small, an inadequate size for a restaurant of this size and stature, Ranleigh thought. As he approached the solitary urinal, the crunching sound emanating from the adjacent stall ceased. The sound resembled someone crushing candy with a hammer. Intrigued, Ranleigh took his time, waiting for any further signs of life from the stall, and just as Ranleigh was running cold water into the sink, a long desperate snort followed by a sigh emanated from the stall.

As he dried his hands, the stall door swung open, revealing a man roughly his age. Wiping his nose with the back of his hand, the man nodded in Ranleigh's direction, revealing the white powder caked around his nostrils.

"Morning," the man said, deliberately averting his gaze from Ranleigh.

"It's afternoon," Ranleigh replied.

"Is it?"

"It is."

"I see," the man said.

The man sported a large black corduroy jacket and loose-fitting brown pants. His brown hair was slicked back from his forehead, and his eyes appeared red-rimmed and lifeless.

"Have you seen Marty around? He told me he'd meet me

here at noon, but he hasn't shown. He's not answering his pages. Any idea when he might show?" the man inquired.

"Sorry, I don't know anyone named Marty, but there's a man downstairs by the bar," Ranleigh responded.

"Fat guy? Looks like a frog?"

"That's him," Ranleigh confirmed.

"Nah, that's not Martin. That guy's a pimp. He sits there all day while the girls parade in and out, and he's got the cops paid off."

"Sorry then, can't help you," Ranleigh said, turning to leave the washroom.

"Just as well, I guess," the man murmured. "I told myself last night that that was it. I can't fucking do this anymore. I swore up and down this morning that I was finished with this shit, and yet, here I am, waiting around again for that piece of shit, Marty." The man's hands were shaking. "Listen, do me a favour, will ya? If you see Marty down there, just let him know I'm looking for him. Would you do that?"

Without waiting for a response, the man retreated into the stall, presumably to start the cycle over again until he could get his hands on Marty. As Ranleigh prepared to leave, he wondered if the man would ever get himself out of that toilet.

Opening the washroom door, he could just make out the crying, masked by the crunching sounds.

PART FOUR

INSOMNIA

CHAPTER 22

Jimmy didn't want to go. His mother dragged him down the hallway, gripping the scruff of his pale blue spring jacket. It was January 1980, and he was long overdue for a winter coat. The sleeves rode too high above his wrists, and the zipper strained whenever he attempted to close it over his already sizeable stomach. Frustrated, he had given up on zipping it altogether, no matter how cold it was outside, preferring to leave the jacket open. Besides, it looked cooler that way.

Sometimes, he worried about the possibility of a bad case of the *bite* as his grandfather called frostbite, if he left it unzipped, but the *bite*, sounded a whole lot better to Jimmy than the *zip*. The thought of catching his stomach while attempting to zip up made him feel queasy. The idea of having to unzip the metal teeth through his skin to free himself made him feel faint.

The burn unit was located in the far eastern section of the hospital's east wing, as far away as possible from the admissions desk, emergency room, and the general day-to-day business of healing the sick. The *medical* reason for this was evident: any type of infection posed a severe threat to burn patients. Jimmy would learn about other reasons before dinnertime.

Escorted by a friendly, yet unnervingly pale nurse, Jimmy and his mother were led to a sliver of a waiting room. The nurse promised to return shortly with gowns and masks, which Jimmy found kind of cool. Having watched a lot of doctor shows on television, he liked the idea of playing dress-up for the afternoon. Quincy was his favourite. After what seemed like forever for Jimmy, the nurse reappeared carrying two sets of blue gowns, matching masks, caps, and mesh pullover slippers. She instructed them to follow her to the sanitizing station, which was just an oversized sink with long handles that looked like chrome hockey sticks to Jimmy.

Jimmy got into it. He rolled up his sleeves and scrubbed his forearms halfway up. He made sure to shut off the faucets using his elbows when he finished. The tired nurse complimented him, mustering a smile. "You're a natural, Jimmy," she said.

"Thanks," Jimmy replied. "I watch all the doctor shows on TV. That's where I learned how to do it. You have to pay attention, so you know what you're doing. Quincy is the best, but M*A*S*H is pretty good, too."

"Well, it certainly shows," she said, leading them back down the hallway.

The nurse came to a stop in front of an oversized door. Jimmy could hear a machine running rhythmically on the other side. The nurse addressed Jimmy, explaining that children were rarely allowed in the burn unit due to patient safety concerns. However, his mother had insisted on bringing him to visit today. *Was that a grin*, thought the nurse, as she nodded in the mother's direction?

The nurse continued, "I must admit, I was personally against it, but the hospital administrator overruled me, and well, here you are."

Jimmy felt uneasy, but wanting to appear doctor-like, he nodded his head and muttered under his breath, "Yes, nurse. I see."

"Now, Jimmy, your aunt is a fighter, and she has good and bad days. Today has been a good day so far, but I must warn you, she won't look at all like the person you remember," the nurse cautioned.

Jimmy thought to himself, *I don't have the foggiest idea, what my aunt looks like.* His knowledge of her was limited to the hushed conversations between his parents. He knew she was a heavy drinker, and often made friends with bad men who beat her up. She always needed money, and his mother had banned her from coming to their house.

His last memory of her was a night when she showed up at their door, banging loudly and begging to be let in. She was yelling and crying, but his mother refused to open the door, threatening to call the police. After the yelling finally stopped, Jimmy's mother went back to the kitchen and finished up the dishes.

During the bus ride to the hospital, Jimmy's mother revealed that his aunt had been hospitalized numerous times over the years, and she had stopped visiting her. That she couldn't take it. The black eyes, the broken noses needing to be reset, the stitches, and the concussions. But this time was different.

As the sun warmed Jimmy's face through the bus window, his mother leaned closer and whispered, quieter than he thought she was capable of, that his aunt was going to die. She had staggered back to her motel room, collapsed on the couch, lit a cigarette, and passed out.

Firefighters arrived and managed to rescue her, rushing her to the hospital. Jimmy would later wish they hadn't, that it would have been better if they had just left her in there to die. The sound of her screams haunted the firefighters for weeks. She was brought to the hospital "just in time," according to his mother. She hadn't been expected to survive the night.

Because his aunt was going to die and die sober (if you didn't count the morphine), his mother believed it was the Christian thing to do for Jimmy to see her one last time and say goodbye, or at least that's what Jimmy thought.

With all this new information swirling in his head, Jimmy was dragged out of school and into the hospital that January afternoon, wearing his pale blue jacket. What his mother hadn't told him was that his aunt, when she was younger, had a beautiful laugh and a mischievous sense of humour and was radiant. She was crowned homecoming queen in high school and had a soft spot for underdogs of the world and always stood up for them. It was this woman who lay dying in the burn unit, but Jimmy would never know any of that.

What Jimmy saw that afternoon would haunt him for the rest of his life.

The nurse issued a final warning. "Don't touch her, stay far away from the bed, and if you feel sick to your stomach, please go straight to the bathroom, right here. I also ask that you keep your visit brief. As I mentioned, she's having a better day, but that can change rapidly." She pushed open the door. It looked heavy.

CHAPTER 23

Life had returned to normal for Leigh Meeks. He no longer struggled to afford food and walking to work was a thing of the past. Even Jimmy had reverted to his usual, irritating self, and the incident with the gun, forgotten. Dodging the building superintendent had become a routine part of Leigh's day, and as expected, the first notice of non-payment of rent had slipped under his door.

Leigh knew that the notices would soon become more threatening and more legal. He calculated that he had just enough time to get the rent check in before ending up on the street. Despite the anxiety this caused him, Leigh felt lighter and happier than he had in years. He cared less about work and was content to work at Crystal's pace. He even didn't mind wearing the name badge.

The dreams persisted, and Leigh settled into his new dream life, savouring each moment in the new reality. It seemed that he had found a way out of the *trap*. As long as he could spend his days in the dream place, he believed he could endure anything that the nights dealt him. For the first time in his life, Leigh felt a sense of gratitude.

The only threat to his newfound freedom was the challenge of balancing his two lives. Since the new world had opened up to him, he longed to spend as much time there as possible. He had become obsessed with it and desired to stay longer but could never manage it. He couldn't sleep longer than his job would allow if he wanted to keep a roof over his head. He understood that he needed a safe place to sleep to keep the other world alive.

Late one night in the lunchroom, while contemplating this, he even wondered if death might release him to the dream place permanently. No, those thoughts were not sane, and best be avoided altogether. Pragmatism and moderation were the only things that would sustain the dream place. And that's when the trouble began.

I apologize for not writing in a while. Things have improved for me, and life has settled down a bit. I'm sorry if you were worried. I realize my last letter may have sounded desperate, but the good news is that I still have a job and have managed to hang on to the apartment.

I'm happy to report that the dreams continue and are better than ever. However, there has been an interesting development. I have discovered that the dreams continue on their own even after I wake up. Last week, while walking along Cumberland Street, I decided to have a drink at Hemingway's, a restaurant near my apartment. It was 2 PM, and I knew I was cutting it close, but I thought I had enough time. The bar was lively, and after two beers, I lost track of time. Before I could pay the bill and get out of there, I woke up in my real apartment in a full-blown panic attack. The next day, I went back to Hemingway's to investigate. I asked the bartender how long I had stayed and if I had paid my bill. She told me that I settled up with her and left around four-thirty.

I continue to talk to Charlotte on the phone, but we still haven't met. In our last conversation, she mentioned reading the latest draft of the novel I've submitted and that she loves it. She thinks it's my best one yet. She wants to discuss it over dinner as she plans to return to Toronto for a family matter.

We've made plans to meet at Massimo's on Bay at eight, which is a short walk for me. It seems I've got myself in quite a jam. Fortunately, I have Sunday night off, so that's not the problem. The problem is: I need to figure out how to stay asleep in my apartment past 8 PM. I don't know how I am going to manage it, but I intend to be there.

Love,
Leigh

Leigh had weekends off, courtesy of Crystal. Ever since he gained this perk long before the dreams, he had attempted to reverse his sleep schedule on Saturdays and Sundays, but he quickly abandoned the idea. It was too hard on his system. He was certain there must be a labour law preventing employers from scheduling continuous overnight shifts, but he was equally certain that PackUcan had found a way around it. Besides, who would speak up? Hadn't his rebellion against the badges nearly rendered him homeless? It made him wonder what Blaireau would do to the poor sap who went as far as reporting them—she'd probably have him shot.

Truth be told, Leigh didn't mind the overnights too much. He had gotten used to it and wasn't particularly jazzed about switching back to working days. However, the downside was that when the weekend rolled around, Leigh found himself awake all night with little to do. He didn't know anyone who worked nights outside of the warehouse, and the thought of socializing with Jimmy or Ron was out of the question, no matter how lonely he felt.

Almost immediately, Leigh regretted telling Charlotte that he would be able to meet her for dinner. It was a problem he hadn't anticipated. Meeting her in person had become a mild obsession for him, so it was no surprise that he had eagerly accepted the opportunity. Now he just had to figure out a way to sleep a little longer than usual on Sunday night. That was all.

Shouldn't be a problem, Leigh thought. He only needed to sleep an extra four hours at most. And if he failed to sleep in, wouldn't dream Ranleigh find his way to Massimo's on Bay without his conscious participation, just like he did at Hemingway's?

Leigh also considered the possibility that the dream might not continue on the newly altered trajectory that he himself had set. The thought of Charlotte sitting alone at the restaurant, wondering why he hadn't shown up and why he wasn't answering his phone, made him uneasy. He needed to find a way to knock himself out for an extra four hours and thought he might have a solution.

CHAPTER 24

There existed precisely eight parking spaces, with two designated for visitors, situated in diagonal cutouts directly in front of the building. All of them were taken. Ranleigh maneuvered his shiny sports car around the back and parked directly in front of the warehouse entrance. Having grown accustomed to seeing the building only at night, he had forgotten what a wretched shithole it truly was.

As he killed the engine, he wondered why the visitor spots were occupied. Who, in their right mind, would ever *visit* a place like this, anyway? Opening the car door, he figured that a couple of front office employees must have taken the liberty of claiming those spots for themselves. No backroom worker would dare park there, and besides, none of them could afford cars.

Lighting a cigarette, Ranleigh resisted the habitual urge to enter through his usual backdoor entrance. Leaning on the hood, he thought of Jimmy, wondering what he would think. Maybe he should drop by and say hello once he was done.

Kicking an empty plastic container bearing the words "Instant Coffee" on its front, which reminded him of his waking life, Ranleigh torpedoed his cigarette almost making a direct hit with a torn condom wrapper. Buttoning his overcoat, he made his way down the driveway at the side of the building toward the front doors of PackUcan.

As Ranleigh approached the front door, a minor flutter of anxiety rumbled in his belly, suggesting that this might be a very bad idea. The receptionist would instantly recognize him, wonder who the fuck was he kidding in that expensive suit, and believe that his charade of his would cost him his job. But, of course, that couldn't happen here.

The receptionist turned away from the computer screen, visibly surprised. She quickly straightened her skirt, giving Ranleigh the warmest, *welcome to PackUcan smile* you ever saw in your life, assuming one had ever found reason enough to park in the visitor's spot. Stomping the snow off his shoes, Ranleigh said, "Good morning. I noticed that the parking spots in front were full, so I parked around the back. I hope that's all right." She blushed, slightly embarrassed. "Yes, of course, that's perfectly fine. Normally, we, uh, would have a spot available for you, but it has been a rather busy morning here," she lied. Ranleigh turned to look at the empty lobby, sensing her discomfort.

"How can I assist you this morning, Mister...? Have you been here before?"

This caught him off guard. He took a deep breath to brace himself. Here goes, he thought.

"The name's Meeks, Ranleigh Meeks, and I need to speak with someone in your sales department."

"I knew it!" she squealed. "I thought it was you when you came in. I'm a huge fan. I've read everything you've ever written. I can't believe it! Wait until I tell the girls."

Leaning forward over the counter, she displayed her cleavage for Ranleigh, the same woman who not too long ago had regarded him with contempt and disgust. As she leaned in, resting her breasts on the countertop, Ranleigh caught a whiff of a noxious blend of the cheap coffee he had never been offered, cheaper perfume, and stale cigarettes. The smell forced him to lean back. He couldn't help feeling a little sorry for her. *We are all looking for a way out of the trap*, he thought.

"Do you have an appointment, Mr. Meeks?"

"Please, it's Ranleigh. Do I need one? Listen, if everyone here is too busy to see me..."

"Don't be silly! Sales, you said. They'll be thrilled to have a celebrity in the place. You know, we might even have a shipment of your new book in the back. I hate to ask, but would you mind signing one for me on your way out? If it's not too much trouble."

"It would be my pleasure," Ranleigh said.

She took his coat and hung it on the empty rack. In his overconfidence, Ranleigh almost led the way down the hall to the large boardroom just beyond the reception. Quickly recovering, he stepped aside, signaling for her to take the lead. Despite rejecting her painfully obvious come-on, Ranleigh couldn't help but sneak a glance at her behind.

They passed by Blaireau's office. She sat there, staring blankly at the computer screen, oblivious to the peculiar visitor heading past her and toward the boardroom.

"Please, have a seat, and I'll be right back. Can I get you anything? Coffee?"

"A coffee would be great," Ranleigh said.

The large boardroom was small. The rectangular table had seen better days, and the chair was upholstered in scratchy, grey fabric that reminded Ranleigh of a sky that hadn't seen sunlight in a long time. Near his pant leg, he noticed a deep, brown stain that someone had tried hard to scrub out. The walls were bare, the colour of plumber's putty.

Ranleigh didn't have to wait long. A man yanked open the door and barreled into the room, celebrity worship shining through bloodshot eyes marinating in alcohol. Ranleigh didn't recognize him. The man extended his hand, which was shaking noticeably. He was a terrible actor.

"Thank you for making the trip this morning. It's not every day we have a real live celebrity in the office," he said. "My name's Jerry Jones, but all my friends call me Jonesy."

"Ranleigh Meeks. Thanks for seeing me on such short notice," Ranleigh replied.

"Anytime," Jonesy said, taking his seat directly across from Ranleigh.

Opening a leather notebook, the man said, "Stop me if you've heard this one before: What do you call it when one blonde blows into another blonde's ear?" He didn't wait for a response. "Data transfer," he chuckled at his joke.

Ranleigh maintained his poker face, which caught Jonesy a bit off guard. After an uncomfortable silence, Jonesy broke it with, "So, what can I do for you this morning, Mr. Meeks? I can't for the life of me figure out why a man of your stature would even be aware of this place's existence."

"It's my understanding that your company handles distribution for mid-sized suppliers of books, CDs, CD-ROMs and DVDs. Is that correct?"

"Correct. If it's distribution you're looking for, you've come to the right place. Maybe you're doing research? I saw that movie of yours about the Mafia. Loved it! Why don't we head across the road for a cocktail, and I can answer any questions?" Ranleigh glanced at his watch - it was just past eleven.

"A little early for me."

"Busy schedule, huh?" Jonesy said, ignoring Ranleigh's response. The receptionist tapped on the glass door before entering with the coffee.

"Excuse me, gents. Mr. Meeks, here's your coffee," she said, placing the mug in front of him on the table. "If there's anything else you need, give me a holler. I'm just down the hall."

"Thanks, Phyl," Jonesy said, giving her a lecherous once over. With the door closed behind her, Jonesy turned back to his leather folder, clicking a ballpoint pen with one hand, and straightening the knot in his loud tie, which featured bright neon fruit on a black background, with the other.

"Before we get started, I'd like to ask you a question," Ranleigh said.

"Shoot."

"I was wondering who's in charge of staffing here. Before I explain the reason for my visit today, I'd like to know a little bit about the operation, you know, from the human angle. I'm curious to know what kind of outfit you run here when it comes to the team you've got working for you in the warehouse, the frontline workers," Ranleigh said.

Ranleigh could tell by Jonesy's expression that the request was unusual, but this whole visit was unusual. Ranleigh hadn't given much thought to how he was going to explain his presence, but Jonesy had provided the perfect opportunity. *Research for a new novel.*

"That would be Blaireau. You passed her office on your way in," he said.

"Any chance you could ask her to join us?" Ranleigh said.

"Sure, she can. Just give me a quick second, I'll go get her."

CHAPTER 25

"Go on. Go on and kiss your aunt like a good boy," his mother commanded after the pretty, tired nurse left the room.

If the smell in the room hadn't been so sickening, bringing Jimmy dangerously close to tossing his breakfast, he would have let out a shriek. This couldn't be his aunt lying in that bed. She looked like a monster to Jimmy. He couldn't take his eyes off the bandages, recalling an old monster movie he had seen on the late show—maybe "The Mummy Returns."

And now his mother wanted him to kiss the monster. His young mind tried to cope with the situation, searching for safe, associations locked in his memory bank. Jimmy thought of the child Pharaoh Tutankhamun. He couldn't know his young mind was attempting to protect him from the potential trauma. It was seeking context for what it saw, trying to find familiarity in the creature before him that he once called aunt.

A tent of white gauzy fabric had been erected over most of her body, sparing him from an outright horror that no amount of context could have saved him from. However, he saw her face—the right side burned beyond recognition. Her bandaged arm stuck out from under the tent, her hand curled inward like a claw, charred, scraped, and oozing.

"Jimmy, mind your mother and go give your aunt a kiss

goodbye," his mother repeated.

"I won't do it."

"What did you say to me?" The refusal had more to do with paralytic fear than standing up to her.

"I won't do it, Momma. Please don't make me!"

"Don't be ridiculous, Jimmy. This is your aunt. She's your flesh and blood. If I say to give her a kiss goodbye, and if you know what's good for you, then, by Jiminy, you will go over there and kiss your aunt goodbye," she hissed. "Don't be a crybaby."

Jimmy saw the hand move. Slight, but deliberate. His mind believed she was trying to comfort him, telling him that it was okay, that he didn't have to if he didn't want to, and for that, he was grateful. Jimmy obeyed and slowly approached the bed, glancing back at his mother. He thought he saw a brief grin flash across her face like a flashbulb—flash!—then gone. But it was there.

The smell of bleach, sulphur, and perfume made Jimmy's head swoon. Determined to mind his mother, he took a couple of shaky steps forward, in sync with the respirator. Standing at the bedside, eyes shut tight, Jimmy leaned forward, puckering his lips, when a hand grabbed his shoulder. Finally, Jimmy did what he had wanted to do since they followed the nurse into the hospital room. He screamed.

"What the hell are you doing?" the nurse yelled, losing her composure. "I thought I told you to stand well back from the patient. It's extremely dangerous to be anywhere near her. An infection could kill her!" She yanked Jimmy back towards his mother, almost lifting him off his feet.

"He wanted to give his beloved aunt a kiss goodbye. Before, you know, *the end*. I tried to stop him, but you know how children can be," his mother said.

"Kiss her?" the nurse repeated, dumbfounded.

"It wasn't me, she—," Jimmy was cut short by the nurse.

"I would like both of you to leave. Immediately." Not only did they pose an extreme danger to her patient, but the nurse also felt, call it nurse's intuition, that something was not right with the mother.

"Not even a few more minutes to say our goodbyes. I'll make sure he stays back here, behind me," Jimmy's mother said to the nurse, snapping her fingers at her son.

"Out!" the nurse said, swinging open the door.

Jimmy bolted for the hall, steadying himself on an abandoned IV pole when he heard his mother say on her way out, "See you around, Sis. I sure hope the Good Lord forgives you. Cause it'll be a hell of a lot hotter where you're headed than that fire you just came out of. And if He doesn't, let's face it, you have only yourself to blame."

"OUT!" the nurse yelled as Jimmy saw his mother saunter out of the room with that grin back on her face.

Memories of that day floated in front of Jimmy as he poked at a stack of pancakes on the table in front of him. Jimmy didn't feel like eating and decided to skip the gym. Quietly scraping the remaining stack of pancakes into the garbage, making sure his mother wouldn't hear, Jimmy felt thick with sadness. He did love his mother, but like the nurse did that day, he knew there was something seriously wrong with her.

CHAPTER 26

Jonesy reluctantly brought Blaireau back to the boardroom to continue the meeting. Blaireau appeared unimpressed by the presence of a celebrity author.

Jonesy, smitten, said, "Perhaps now you could share why you dropped by today. My guess is you're researching a new book, or maybe even a movie. You know who should play me? The guy from that show everyone's talking about, ER. People tell me we could be brothers."

Ignoring the salesman, Ranleigh kept his gaze fixed on Blaireau, relishing her discomfort.

Ranleigh looked directly at Blaireau and asked, "Tell me about those badges."

"These?" she said, looking genuinely confused. "Well, our parent company, located overseas, has a custom of wearing badges at work, over your heart as a sign of respect." *Well done*, Ranleigh thought, impressed by her smooth response.

"Mr. Jones is right. I'm conducting research for a new novel, planning to base my main character on someone who works in a place just like this. I like to get things right. The badges intrigue me, though. I think they'd be a nice touch. So, you wear them when you're public-facing, like in our meeting today, right? And your receptionist, I noticed was wearing one when I came in," Ranleigh continued.

"Yes, exactly," she said, visibly hoping Ranleigh would drop the matter.

"I get it. I kind of like the custom," Ranleigh said, and she smiled her I'm so glad you see things my way, smile. But Ranleigh had more to say.

"Ms. Blaireau, is it?" She nodded. "As the receptionist brought me here, I couldn't help but notice you had the badge on in your office. In fact," Ranleigh said, gesturing toward the glass walls of the boardroom that revealed the entire office. "It looks like everyone here is wearing a badge. Even the custodian over there has one. Do you expect all these people, in such a remote place, to have much, if any, contact with the public today?"

Blaireau's face started turning a light shade of coral. Jerry gallantly intervened, attempting to bail her out. It was at that moment that Ranleigh realized Jonesy was sleeping with her.

"Yes, well, you're absolutely right there, partner. You got us. We all wear the badges all the time, like she said, it's a custom, a sign of respect," Jerry quickly agreed, not wanting to ruin his chance at an autograph or becoming Ranleigh's new research assistant.

"I think it's stupid," Ranleigh declared.

"Oh, I do too," Jonesy said.

"Do you agree, Ms. Blaireau?" Ranleigh asked, and an uncomfortable silence settled in the room. Ranleigh was prepared to wait. He savoured the moment, knowing how many people Blaireau had subjected to similar treatment and worse. Dream or not, this was priceless.

"I see. Let's move on, shall we?" Ranleigh said.

"Yes, let's," Jonesy quickly concurred.

"Mr. Jones," Ranleigh turned to face Jerry.

"Remember, Mr. Meeks, all my friends call me Jonesy," he interjected.

"Sure, you asked me earlier about my research, and I was hoping to find somebody here who could help me with that. Someone who could give me the real inside scoop. I want to understand the mind of the salesman, really get deep inside, and appreciate what makes him tick. My publisher would, of course, pay you for your time, and you'd get a mention in the novel itself. Is that something you might be interested in?" Jonesy was salivating.

"Would I be interested? Of course, I would be. You've come to the right place, Mr. Meeks. If there's one thing I know about, it's sales," Jonesy barked, barely containing himself. "This calls for a celebratory drink," he said, rushing to fetch a bottle from his bottom desk drawer. It was the fastest Ranleigh had seen him move all morning. However, Ranleigh halted him in his tracks.

"I'll pass on the drink. It's a little early in the day for me but thank you." Ranleigh stood up to leave. "But I must say that this badge business is still bothering me. I still don't understand why. If you all know each other and I'm guessing you see each other day after day, then why the badges? And why first and last names?"

Blaireau, who had remained silent, finally spoke up. "They're voluntary," she said, showing a hint of vulnerability.

It seemed Blaireau wasn't entirely immune to the power of celebrity. And if Jonesy could earn some extra money on the side, maybe he'd finally get the balls to leave his wife.

"I beg your pardon?" Ranleigh replied, in total shock.

"They're voluntary. The staff doesn't have to wear them if they don't want to," she lied. "It seems, Mr. Meeks, we have a very committed staff who *love* their jobs."

"I see," Ranleigh responded. "So, if I were to ask you to remove your badge right here and now, without any fear of retribution from management, could you do it? Oh, wait, you are management, but you know what I mean, right?"

A badge hit the table, but it wasn't hers. Jonesy had removed his and tossed it in front of Ranleigh. You're gonna pay for that one, Jonesy-boy, Ranleigh thought.

Taking out his car keys from his pocket, Ranleigh turned to face Blaireau.

"I'll tell you what. I'm prepared to have my publisher send

over a contract for Jerry to sign right now, and I'm also prepared to put in a good word with my publisher about this place. Maybe we can exert some influence and get you a few more contracts for your business. We have good relationships with all the major bookstore chains in Canada and the U.S. Hell, I'll even do a meet and greet with the corporate delegation you have visiting later this month." Jerry Jones nearly wet himself. "However, this is all on one condition. I've been called a bit of an eccentric, and as an eccentric, I reserve the right to make the occasional odd request," Ranleigh paused.

"My condition is this: Ms. Blaireau needs to remove her badge, drop it here on the table alongside yours, and then I'd like her to make an announcement to the staff out there and to the workers in the warehouse. She should remind them that wearing badges is strictly voluntary and that they won't be penalized in any way if they choose not to wear them. If she does that, Mr. Jones, I will call my publisher today. And if she doesn't, no deal and I'll find someone else to help me with my book."

Jerry looked pleadingly at Blaireau, whose makeup was beginning to crack around her lips. This is how it feels, Blaireau. This is how it feels to be humiliated. Both Mr. Jerry Jones and Ranleigh Meeks watched her as she removed her badge and placed it on the boardroom table.

CHAPTER 27

It was still a shock when he reemerged into his real life after coming back down the rabbit hole. It took him a few minutes to acclimatize, and despite the reduced intensity, there was always anxiety present when he opened his eyes. Nevertheless, the intensity was now far less, and the duration was shorter. At three o'clock that afternoon, he woke up on the couch after he visited with Blaireau and Jonesy. He didn't remember falling asleep there. After a few laps around the kitchen table, he got dressed and headed out to get the supplies he would need to remain asleep during his dinner with Charlotte.

His first stop was a walk-in clinic not far from his apartment. Leigh couldn't recall the last time he had seen a doctor or a dentist. Leigh had gone through this routine once years before, during a particularly difficult period with his anxiety.

A psychologist who bore a striking resemblance to Sigmund Freud only with less hair, had suggested he see a doctor to obtain a prescription. Normally, Leigh would have avoided pills, but his panic attacks had been severe and were interfering with his ability to hold a job, so he eventually gave in.

He discovered that the prescribed pills were not meant to manage day-to-day nervousness. They were to be taken only if he found himself on the verge of a full-blown panic attack. To manage his anxiety disorder, he would have to go on Prozac long-term. In the event of an attack, he was advised to take one pill immediately to stave off a potentially ruinous crisis. The pills were to be taken only in emergencies.

The doctor informed him that the rest of his anxiety issues could be dealt with in therapy. For the price of one hundred dollars per hour, three hours a week, Leigh could expect significant progress in six months to a year. Leigh pocketed the pills and never went back. He had used them on two occasions, but when the first pill didn't work, he took a second one, which knocked him out cold. The second time, Leigh had slept for nearly fourteen hours and, ironically, nearly lost his job anyway. He flushed the rest down the toilet.

The waiting room of the clinic was half full, mostly with small children suffering from colds, a few elderly patients with God-knows-what, and a kid with what appeared to be a broken arm. Leigh thought, *maybe the cast is coming off today.*

The nurse called him in quickly, interrupting his reading of an article about the O.J. Simpson defense. Leigh gave the doctor a well-rehearsed speech about the nature and severity of his panic attacks, leaving out the laps around the kitchen table. The doctor checked his blood pressure, listened to his heart, had him take a few deep breaths, and scribbled something on a pad. He tore off the white square page and handed it to Leigh.

"I'm giving you a prescription for twenty Ativan. These pills are powerful and are only meant to be used in the event of an attack. My advice is to carry them with you. Twenty should last you a while. They can be addictive, so if I see you back here in a few days asking for more, the ones you have will be your last. Understand?" Leigh nodded. "Good. And quit smoking."

The doctor removed his latex gloves with a snap and a flash of powder, like a magic trick, and dropped them in the bin. He bid Leigh a good day and left him to gather his things. Leigh wondered if this is how prostitutes felt. Probably.

"The fucking music needs to be turned down," Jimmy hissed into the phone.

"What?"

"I said turn off the fucking music."

"Oh, sure," Leigh slurred, spitting. Reaching for the volume, he accidentally knocked over his drink, and the liquid rolled across the table like gathering storm clouds. "Shit." Jimmy shook his head as the volume lowered.

"Bedder?" Leigh asked.

"Yeah, it's better. Why the fuck are you calling me at this hour? Are you wasted?"

"I might have had one or two, what's it to ya?"

"What's it to *me*? You called me. You're just lucky you didn't wake my mother."

"Yeah. Yeah. Listen, Jimmy. I just wanted to call you and say it's okay about the gun. It's okay. I get it. I get you," Leigh slurred. "I think you're all right, man. When I first started at the warehouse, I thought you were a proper tit, but you know what? You're all right, Jimmy."

"And you're way too fucked up. Listen, Leigh, sleep it off. You've got to work on Monday."

"Yeah, yeah," Leigh said. "Hey, Jimmy?"

"What?"

"Do you dream?"

"Of course, I dream. Everybody dreams."

"Well, that's where you're wrong, muchacho. Not everybody dreams, you fucking idiot. I never did. Well, only once. But now I do. Now I dream every day. I'm dreaming all the time."

"Well, congratulations. And go fuck yourself, Leigh. I'm hanging up."

"Okay. Okay. Sorry," Jimmy heard Leigh light a cigarette on the other end of the phone.

"Just one more thing and I'll let you go," Leigh said.

"Go to bed, Leigh. And promise you'll put that thing out now," Jimmy said urgently.

"Yeah, yeah."

"Promise?"

"Yeah," Leigh said. "But here's my question, Jimmy-boy. What I really want to know is this. Do you think it's possible to carry things from here into a dream? You know, from here to there. What do you think, Jimmy? I know you can't be as stupid as you look."

"Fuck you, Leigh," Jimmy hung up the phone.

BANG. SLAP. BANG. Arrhythmic sounds. Leigh's head rested on the cool surface of the wooden door, slapping it with his right hand. Full hand, heel hand, full hand, heel hand.

"Come on, you fucker. I know you're in there," Leigh yelled.

A few curious neighbours poked their early Sunday morning heads out into the hallway.

"Meeks. Fuck off and go home," the Superintendent of the building yelled back from the other side of his door. "If you don't knock it off, I'm calling the cops."

"Come on. No need to call the police, my good man. I just want you to know that although I'm late on the rent, I have no intention of paying it. Not now! Not ever!" Bang. Slap. Bang. "You got me? Never." Leigh's forehead pivoted counterclockwise on the door, causing a mouthful of drool to leak onto the floor.

"Whoops," Leigh said.

He was beginning to feel a sinking sensation in his chest. He had remembered to take the pills. About half an hour before his call to Jimmy, he had awkwardly settled down on the couch, spilling a good portion of his drink. He popped the lid with some difficulty and fished out two chalky white oval pills, *like miniature Easter eggs*, he thought and placed them on his tongue. Then he drained what was left in his glass to get them down.

He should have stayed put. He probably would have been in the dream place by now, but he had a question for Jimmy and then got it into his head that he was being treated unfairly. By everybody. And he needed to do something about it.

But now he found himself in the hallway, sinking downwards to oblivion. He still had enough of his faculties to know that if he didn't make it back to the relative safety of his apartment, he would risk missing Charlotte at the restaurant, and all his planning would be for naught. He just couldn't seem to move his feet, and he was sinking fast. If he passed out in the hallway after this outburst, an ambulance or the police would surely be called. Somebody would have to call, wouldn't they? And if they did, somebody would eventually wake him up, and he would blow the pick-up time.

Using the strength he had left, Leigh lifted one foot from the murky pattern of the carpet, trying to shake off nonexistent muck. He tried to draw some power from the cool surface of the door with his forehead.

"Meeks! Get away from my door or else," the Super threatened.

"I'm going. I'm going," Leigh offered as his hand slid down the door. He wasn't going to make it. He couldn't see and couldn't feel his legs. Just as his knees began to buckle, he felt a hand grab his wrist and place his arm across a shoulder.

"Here, lean on my shoulder," a voice he didn't recognize said. He leaned heavily on the support and was maneuvered back to his apartment. Once inside, someone dragged him down the hall to his bedroom and pitched him forward onto the bed. The last thing he was aware of in this world was the click of the latch as his apartment door closed.

I have no way of knowing whether these letters are reaching you. I'm posting two letters a week and I am sure that I have the correct address. As you haven't written back, I'm only to assume that you either haven't received them or you choose not to respond. Nevertheless, I'm not going to stop.

I waited at the restaurant for her, but she never showed.

My passage to the dream place that morning was the smoothest so far.

However, there was one notable difference—I had lost an hour. Up until that point, all transitions had been instantaneous, aside from the sensation of falling. It felt like descending a well, anticipating the bottom. Yet, this time, darkness was the only thing I encountered. It must have been the pills. Consequently, instead of waking up in my dream bed at 9 AM, the clock read 10 AM.

My experience in the dream place today was more vivid than ever before. Also, maybe the pills? I felt stronger and even more at peace. The colours appeared more brilliantly, and the sounds harmonized as I moved through the streets. In the mid-afternoon, a sense of drowsiness began to set in, which caused me slight concern. I considered lying down for a while, without considering why I might be tired. However, I decided to grab a coffee, thinking it would wake me up. Unfortunately, it didn't. Additionally, I heard loud banging originating from a direction I couldn't pinpoint. It persisted on and off for approximately five minutes before abruptly stopping. It sounded like somebody banging on a door.

Later that evening, I had nearly given up hope when the phone in my pocket rang. Stepping outside the restaurant's front doors onto Bay Street, I answered. It was Charlotte, and our conversation went something like this:

"Ranleigh?"

"Hey."

"How are you?"

"Fine. And you?"

"I'm okay. I've decided to stay here another night and wanted to call you again in case you try to reach me later but can't. Are you outside? It sounds loud where you are."

"Yes, I'm on my way to grab something to eat. Is everything all right?"

"As good as can be expected. I'm trying to support him, but visiting day is just too depressing. I won't bore you with the details. Listen, I won't have time to meet up. I'm catching a flight back to New York tomorrow."

"Sure."

"Thanks, Ranleigh. You got my earlier message, right? It sounded

like you might have. Never mind."

"Have a good night."

"You too and enjoy your dinner. Sorry again for cancelling."

She hung up, and I headed home. On the way, I checked my voicemail and indeed, she had left a message earlier to say that she wouldn't be able to meet for dinner. I'm not sure how I missed it. Despite feeling bitterly disappointed, as you can imagine, I was happy about one thing—it was 8:45 PM when I answered her call. The experiment worked.

Love,
Leigh

CHAPTER 28

The hooks were in, and the drugs were working their way deeper into the soft, fleshy underside of his mind and body. A time would come when wriggling off the line would be impossible. He now oriented himself totally in the direction of the dream place, a fuck you, about-face from his existence. He was determined to protect the dreams at any cost, willing to starve for them and die for them. He would do anything to keep the dreams alive, except the one thing that might have guaranteed success, but who could say? He would fail to save himself and instead throw himself to the wolves.

Despite his best efforts to ration the tablets, the pills were running out. He had set a strict rule: *for weekend use only*. Hoping to have more time in the dream place on weekends and a chance to meet Charlotte, he saved the pills. But that still meant four pills per weekend. If he hadn't been losing his capacity for honesty with himself, he would have realized that he had dipped into the bottle once or twice outside the ironclad schedule. The bottle initially contained twenty pills, and they were rapidly depleting.

Sometimes they talked in the afternoon, while other times she took flights to God-knows-where. On Saturday and Sunday nights, he managed to remain in the dream place until

11 PM. Afterward, he would spend the rest of the night hiding in his apartment. Leigh had become obsessed with meeting Charlotte, although asking personal questions about her whereabouts during her personal time was inappropriate according to the dream place's rules. Nevertheless, he was determined to find out.

Day-to-day life became increasingly intolerable. Leigh still managed to get to work, mostly on time. When he refrained from taking pills, he resorted to drinking, resulting in him being late on three occasions. He had handled the spectacle with the Superintendent but just barely. He was now three months behind in rent, and the once-feared notices were accumulating under his door at an alarming rate.

Mistakes started to occur at work, ones he would never have made before the dreams. Labels were attached to the wrong boxes, orders were mixed up, or left incomplete. In one instance, he botched things so badly that a formal complaint was filed and tracked back to him. He had sent a truck full of DVDs not only to the wrong address but to the wrong province, prompting an investigation by Blaireau.

Leigh became even more uncommunicative than usual. Instead of socializing, he did everything possible to sleep during breaks. He found this brief respite to be the only thing keeping him from quitting altogether.

He would rest his head on a table in the break room and drift off for fifteen or twenty minutes. During that time, he would awaken in his bed in what he now called home, or sit in the dark living room, and smoke a cigarette. Soon, he would feel the pull of sleep, dragging him down like holding a heavy rock while treading water. Eventually, exhaustion would take over, and he would sink to the bottom. No matter how hard he fought, he would end up back in the break room, each time more heartbreaking than the last.

Leigh's drunken call to Jimmy had the unintended consequence of bringing them closer together, at least from Jimmy's perspective. He understood that Leigh had reached out in a time of need, and it didn't matter a lick to Jimmy that

Leigh was, for the most part, *pretending* to avoid him. They were friends, and Jimmy would be there for him. And he was.

Blaireau had it out for Leigh, and Jimmy couldn't fathom why. Maybe there didn't need to be a reason. People didn't always need a reason to hold a grudge against someone. His mother, case in point. Lately, Blaireau seemed to be on a mission and left additional instructions for Jimmy beyond the usual list.

Most of these instructions revolved around Leigh. Blaireau wanted to know when Leigh took breaks and for how long, if he slept on the job, and if he showed any signs of substance abuse. The punch cards were available for her to review at any time. Jimmy had no control over that, and there were limits to what he would do to help his friend. However, white lies were acceptable to Jimmy, especially if they prevented Leigh from losing his job. If Leigh had known how many times Jimmy had saved him from termination in the past few weeks, he wouldn't have treated him the way he did. But Jimmy understood that Leigh needed him, and that's all Jimmy had ever wanted: to be needed.

CHAPTER 29

"This no fucking tea party," growled the Russian.

Jimmy introduced him as Stan, but the man flanking his right side called him Stas. Leigh suspected it was short for Stanislav, but he couldn't be sure. The pills had run out, leaving Leigh with few other options. He had tried several clinics to replenish his supply, but they only provided him with five pills at a time, and he could only visit them once. After exhausting his options at the clinics, Leigh returned to the first doctor but was met with a flat no. The doctor had warned him that he wouldn't prescribe any more pills, regardless of the excuse, and he kept his word.

Leigh tried using over-the-counter sleep aids and cold and flu medications, with and without alcohol. However, they only intensified his anxiety levels and made him vomit. He couldn't sleep and would be sketchy for hours on end.

Leigh had given up on limiting his pill experiments to weekends. He discovered that alcohol when consumed in large enough quantities, dulled his anxiety during the week. So, the question that followed him like a lost puppy looking for a home was, why wait until the weekend? Despite the anxiety, the real problem that required his immediate attention was his lack of pills.

Attempting to crawl into the dream place and stay there longer using alcohol alone was threatening his job. What he felt he needed, what would solve the problem and get things back on track were more sedatives. He had promised himself that if he could just get one more prescription, he would use them sparingly and only on weekends. He promised himself that he would not drink during the week and that he would turn things around at work. He promised himself that he would pay his rent and eat more regularly if he could only get one more bottle of pills.

What had begun innocently enough as an experiment in what Leigh liked to think of as *sleep research* was threatening to take a sudden and hard left into a full-blown problem. But if it didn't interfere with the dream place Leigh could have cared less. And besides, there was the more immediate problem that required his full attention. He was out of pills.

It took a few late-night heart-to-heart conversations at work with Jimmy to persuade him to help. Jimmy didn't need much convincing since he enjoyed their increased interactions. Leigh suspected that Jimmy had obtained his firearm illegally and figured that the person who supplied him with the gun might also have access to the pills he needed. Leigh was more right than he knew.

Occasionally, a person could stumble upon an idea so obvious that it eliminated all obstacles in its power and simplicity, reducing a convoluted path to a single step. The step in this case was named Stas.

As it turned out, Jimmy and Stas met late one night at a 24-hour gym near Leigh's new apartment, the Colonnade. Walking down Yonge Street just blocks away from where he spent half of his time, felt strange for Leigh. He had to be cautious not to confuse the timelines or he might be liable to try and get into the apartment that was only his in his dreams.

The gym occupied the second floor of a building on the corner of Yonge and Charles Streets, directly above a McDonald's and a few doors down from a strip club. While that area south of Bloor Street on Yonge had been run-down and seedy for years, a couple of blocks up and over would lead you to the prestigious area of Yorkville.

In the 1960s, Yorkville was a haven for hippies, prompting one city councilor to suggest hosing down the area to eliminate the smell. However, in the 70s, artists like Neil Young and Joni Mitchell relocated to pursue the American dream (and the American money) in southern California. Yorkville had transformed into the city's destination for the ultra-wealthy, featuring exclusive boutiques and after-hours hangouts catering to wealthy young trust fund preppy kids looking to score cocaine. Now, Yorkville was Leigh's hangout, spending time shopping in boutiques and dining in restaurants that would never have otherwise let him in.

It was obvious to Leigh that Jimmy *loved* Stas. It was also obvious to Leigh that Stas was a dangerous guy. As Jimmy's friend, Stas had the connections to hook Leigh up, but Jimmy had reservations about drugs on moral grounds, so he dragged his feet on the introduction. Guns? Yes. Booze? Sure, occasionally. But drugs? Absolutely not.

Despite his reservations, Leigh managed to convince Jimmy that he was suffering from a severe form of insomnia, which was a contributing factor to his excessive drinking. Leigh tried convincing Jimmy that pills could offer some relief. Jimmy knew about Leigh's drinking problem and his deteriorating mental state. Leigh told Jimmy that the lack of sleep was driving him crazy and that he feared for his sanity. And then he dropped the motherload on him: *Leigh told Jimmy he was afraid he might lose his job.*

Leigh assured Jimmy that he had exhausted all legal channels for obtaining a refillable prescription, but the bastard doctors just accused him of being an addict. An addict, can you imagine? Which Jimmy found funny coming from someone who hadn't showered in days and reeked of alcohol. Despite his respect for doctors, Jimmy couldn't bear losing his only friend at work, or more accurately, his only friend. Assuming that Stas had access to every substance under the sun, Jimmy reluctantly agreed to introduce Leigh to him on the condition that Leigh quit boozing and only use the pills for his sleep problems. Leigh accepted the terms without hesitation.

"Uh yeah, right. Not a tea party. I'll get right to it then," Leigh said, feeling uneasy and exposed in the oversized tank top he had borrowed from Jimmy.

Standing next to Stas, he couldn't help but feel puny. Even Jimmy seemed more physically fit. "Jimmy mentioned you might be able to hook me up. Like, I can score from you," Leigh had never felt more inauthentic in his life (the things people say to get drugs).

Stas turned to Jimmy, his bald head gleaming under the harsh yellow lights. Leigh struggled to locate Stas's neck. Although unfamiliar with steroid use, if Stas wasn't a poster boy for juicing, he didn't know who would be.

"You vouch, Jimmy?" Stas asked, squinting at Jimmy.

"Sure thing, Stan. Leigh's my friend, and I can vouch for him one hundred percent," Jimmy said.

Stas turned back to Leigh, his upper body leading the way.

"Okay, any friend of Jimmy is friend of Stas. What you need?" The relief that flooded through Leigh was clearly visible on his face. Displays like this let guys like Stas know they have you, but Leigh had long given up on maintaining any facade.

"I've been having trouble sleeping," Leigh said.

"Come into my office," Stas said, turning and walking toward the emergency exit.

Jimmy remained where he was. The dimly lit stairwell on the other side of the EXIT door made Leigh feel even more uncomfortable. To create enough space, Leigh had to squeeze past Stas and his henchman, moving a couple of steps down. As he looked up at Stas, he couldn't help but think he looked like a cartoon - the musclebound guy who kicks sand in your face at the beach. Leigh assumed the tanned, massive chest, showcased by the stringed tank top, was a result of countless hours at the gym, visits to the neighbouring tanning salon, and dipping into his own supply. Stas had a tuft of platinum blonde hair atop his head, along with an angry scar that ran diagonally from his forehead, over his nose and disappeared under his jawline.

"So, you need pills?" Stas inquired.

"Yeah, that would be great," Leigh replied. "Sleeping pills."

"Ty che, blyad?!" Stas exclaimed, while his associate grinned. "What the fuck," he clarified for Leigh. "No sleeping pills. Those are for women." Leigh's heart sank in his chest.

"But Stas helps Jimmy's friend. Any friend of Jimmy is a friend of Stas," he said, reaching down to retrieve a bag from a large bulge hidden in his sock, concealed by the white, baggy track pants he wore.

Lifting the bag towards the brightest area of the orange-lit staircase, Stas appeared to weigh its contents with his other meaty hand. Leigh could make out pills, powders, and what seemed to be marijuana, all neatly packaged in tiny Ziplock bags. The pills glittered like illuminated pieces of candy. Stas looked back at Leigh.

"These new. Hot. Hot like Jenny McCarthy. Everybody wants. Oxy. Strong like Ox," he smiled at Leigh, flexed a bicep, and kissed it. "You want sleep? These knock you out, yes?"

"Yes," Leigh replied, and a few minutes later, the deal was done.

Stas was not a licensed physician. Far from it, despite his reputation for efficiency back home with a scalpel. Leigh wasn't sure if he had paid a fair price for the pills, but he was relieved he deferred his rent payment once again, freeing up some cash. One major drawback of buying from the Russian was the lack of instructions on how much to take and when. He offered no advice at all on the matter. He also neglected to inform Leigh about possible side effects and contraindications. On the upside, Leigh now had a refillable prescription that he could fill anytime, day or night, and in any quantity, as long as the cash held.

Hours after parting ways with Jimmy early that Sunday morning, Leigh settled onto the couch and poured himself a drink. Disregarding the promise he had made to Jimmy and with a slight tremor in his right hand, he removed a pill from the baggy given to him by the Russian drug dealer and placed it on the coffee table in front of him.

He felt the rush of complete control that comes at the beginning of a score and wanted to savour it a little while longer. Leigh delicately picked up the Oxy, holding it between his fingers. The pill was round and green, the colour of sick. The pharmaceutical company had stamped the letters "OC" on one side and "80" on the other, presumably indicating the dosage. However, Leigh had no way of knowing whether it was high or low. What if he took too much and overdosed? What if he died? Would the dream place disappear with his life?

Deciding it was too risky, he considered taking half a pill to start and see how it went. He also thought he might lay back on the alcohol a little, but after the ordeal at the gym, he felt he deserved a few drinks to settle his nerves. Besides, he had approximately an hour and a half before he needed to be in his bed, which he now referred to as the *departure lounge*.

Leigh got drunk. He still possessed enough sense to recognize the danger of being inebriated while taking a new pill, but he didn't care. He briefly considered tossing a few pills into his mouth and washing them down with the next drink, but something stopped him cold. Something inside him urged him to forget the whole thing. To forget the dream place, the apartment, Charlotte, the car, the fame, and the money. Just forget the whole damned thing. He thought about flushing the pills and what remained of the alcohol, and maybe trying some good old-fashioned, nose to the grindstone work to get his life back on track.

A voice seemed to say, *You've had your fun, Ranleigh, and now it's time to stop. You can still make something of your life. You don't need to disappear. Wherever you think you're going, it's not real anyway. Let go of it.* Shaking off the voice, Leigh palmed one little green pill and swallowed it, then Leigh was gone.

CHAPTER 30

He had received word that morning that his presence would be required in the front office at the end of his shift, four o'clock sharp. Not exactly like that; more along the lines of, "Hey Meeks. Blaireau wants your ass in her office at four. You must have really fucked up good this time." Crystal, the harbinger of bad news, had been the one to tell him.

Leigh was well aware that Blaireau was summoning him to terminate him. A small part of him wondered why it had taken so long. Ever since the upgrade in his chemical intake, his real life had been rapidly deteriorating—a relentless downward spiral seemingly with no end, until now. However, the dream place was better than ever. In the haze of his confusion, he grasped a notion that the worse it got here, the better it got there. For now, at least. He assumed that there was some law at work. He pondered something like polarity but couldn't be bothered carrying the thought any further.

Initially, Leigh had kept to his promise, reserving pills strictly for weekends. The first time he experienced the transformative effects was revelatory. All pain, and by *all*, I mean every ounce of it, vanished instantly.

Unlike Ativan, which merely buried his anxiety, OxyContin eradicated the pain at its root with a single, sweet chemical tug.

It felt as though a string had been tied around the pain on one end and fastened to a doorknob on the other and slamming that fucker shut, yanked it right out. He coasted on this feeling for half an hour before floating off into a deep and serene slumber. The transition to the dream place occurred instantly on OxyContin. Eyes closed in reality; eyes opened in the place. Simple as that.

During the initial week or two, Leigh managed to hold back, albeit drinking more during the week and disregarding the notices slipped under his door. He stowed them in an old backpack tucked away in the back of his bedroom closet. A reminder of better times. A trip to Europe after high school.

One Saturday, in the hazy state between popping the pills and drifting off, Leigh mustered the courage to open one of the notices. His groggy mind absorbed fragments about a Sheriff and sixty days, but he couldn't connect the dots.

After a few weeks, Leigh discovered that he would wake up from the dream place before he was ready to leave and would need another pill. It happened at odd times - during a phone conversation with Charlotte or while sitting on a bench on Cumberland Avenue smoking a cigarette. A strong urge to sleep in the dream place would wash over him. In an instant, his eyes would open in his real bed, and he would reach out for a pill, struggle to swallow it and fall back asleep.

Because this was happening during the day while sleeping after a shift, Leigh suspected that the light filtering into his room might be the culprit. Attempting to solve the problem, he ventured out and purchased numerous rolls of tin foil, which he painstakingly taped over his apartment windows. But the sleep disturbances continued, leading him to question the pills themselves. Were they the ones waking him up? Were they demanding that he take more? Regardless, they were no longer lasting twelve or thirteen hours. He was now lucky if he got four at a time.

Charlotte's concern grew. Gaps in their conversations and Leigh's frequent nonsensical ramblings prompted her to seek help. She repeatedly implored him to see a doctor and get himself checked out, but he wouldn't. How could he reveal the true cause of his sudden nods? Instead, he tried to assure her that it might be stress-related and would eventually pass. Charlotte suspected narcolepsy.

Leigh had reached a point where he relied on the pills to sleep at all and craved them terribly when awake. He started taking them during work hours, which left him feeling detached. Being late no longer bothered him, and he paid no mind to the sideways glances of his coworkers. His interactions were now limited to Jimmy and the kind-hearted Ron, who listened attentively while loading cardboard into the industrial compactor. Leigh attempted to go through the motions as best he could, but he became increasingly sluggish, and he could feel his grip slipping away.

It was in this state that he found himself back in the reception area of PackUcan, waiting to meet with Blaireau, waiting for the axe to fall. She kept him waiting a long time, and Leigh thought that in the dream place, she wouldn't fucking dare.

A mischievous grin spread across his face. Phyllis, the receptionist, didn't flirt with *this* Leigh. She paid him no attention and sought refuge behind the counter, clacking away on her grimy computer keyboard. Leigh made up his mind that once he returned to the dream place, he would leave a message for Jonesy, demanding the immediate dismissal of Blaireau and Phyllis.

The thought was too funny and brought out a loud, cackling laugh from Leigh. Phyllis halted her typing, only to resume when she felt assured that she was not in any danger. The sound of her typing pounded in his head, triggering the beginnings of a headache. He wondered if he could endure this charade without popping another pill, but he doubted it.

"Hey, you. You can go in now," Phyllis said, displaying no interest in taking him back. Leigh wondered if it was his smell.

"Thanks, Phyl," Leigh muttered as he rose from his seat. Shuffling towards the door, he removed the badge from his shirt and dropped it in the trash can.

Peering down the hallway, Leigh reached into his pocket and retrieved another pill. He deemed this meeting to be a two-pill job but figured it would be best to behave himself. Bringing his hand to his mouth as if stifling a cough, Leigh swallowed the pill. It was then that he spotted a familiar face at the far end of the corridor.

Ron had to pass by Blaireau's office door as he made his way to intercept Leigh. Initially, Blaireau had contemplated assigning Jimmy to the task but killed the idea outright. Over the past few months, Jimmy and Leigh had become closer. She didn't trust Jimmy to carry out the job effectively. Besides, Jimmy was about as much a security guard as she was a Miss Canada contestant. At least Ron possessed a formidable size and Blaireau knew that Ron would never defy her. Never. No, Ron would do nicely. She had observed Ron's interactions with Meeks and believed the gentle giant would have a better chance of talking him down should he go completely postal, which was a real concern given the circumstances. And if persuasion failed, Ron would have no trouble physically ejecting him from the building. Meeks looked like he could barely stand on the best of days.

Leaving her building that morning, Blaireau was greeted by an early preview of the summer that was still months away. Beads of sweat spread across her forehead looking like a swath of bubble wrap. In the mere twenty feet it took to reach her car, she was drenched. Perhaps she would have stayed drier had she dressed more appropriately for the weather anomaly, however, she refused to dress down just because of these newly approved *Casual Fridays* imposed by corporate. And she would certainly never come to work dressed like that slut Phyllis stationed out front.

Blaireau was already planning to reprimand her for yet another dress code violation. Hadn't she made it crystal fucking clear that tank tops and shorts so revealing the delivery guys could see her hoochie were strictly prohibited? Unfortunately, Blaireau happened to have reliable information that the general manager had been receiving regular hookups from Phyllis, going down on him in his car after hours, making it impossible for Blaireau to even broach the subject of getting rid of her. But humiliating her with yet another writeup was strictly Blaireau's domain. She pondered what kind of hooker gear SyPhyllis would be wearing as she cranked up the air conditioning in her car.

The day was destined to be a scorcher. As Blaireau waited for her car to cool down, she felt stifled. So stifled that she sometimes felt like she was choking. Sometimes she felt like she wasn't getting enough air and would run her nails down her neck causing bright red lines to form like faults. The cracks in her composure were starting to show. She was suffocating in the job.

No matter how hard she tried to be fair, people just took advantage. Didn't they realize she was put in this position because she knew what might be best for them? Had it never occurred to them that if they simply followed along, everything would be fine? That they could all breathe freely again?

Her affair with Jerry also left her feeling stifled. He would never leave his wife and family like he promised he would. Their afternoon rendezvous at the Seahorse Motel on Lakeshore had become a tiresome chore. Did she not have enough responsibilities already? The mere thought of it lately made her feel sick.

Today's responsibility involved getting rid of that waste of sperm, Leigh Meeks. He had given her enough grief during his tenure with the company. He thought he was too good for everyone, including her. That his shit didn't stink. Well, she had some news for him, buddy-boy. Not only would his shit stink today, but it's going to hit the proverbial fan and splatter back all over him. Perhaps a good old-fashioned firing squad would wipe that shit-eating grin off his face for good.

Yes, today was going to be a good day.

As Ron approached, Leigh discreetly swallowed the pill, mimicking a cough.

"Hello, young man," Ron said.

"Hey, Ron," Leigh mumbled, feeling the effects of the pill.

With his eyes closed, Leigh wobbled, but an enormous hand steadied him.

"Easy there, Leigh," Ron said.

"Thanks, Ron. I'm feeling a bit under the weather," Leigh lied.

"You could say that," Ron agreed with a nod. "But maybe not in the way *you mean*." A brief and uncomfortable pause followed. Ron took his hand from Leigh's shoulder. "Word is you're getting your walking papers today."

"Yep. Afraid so," Leigh said, the reality of his situation attempting to hammer through the chemical shield he had constructed. "But I'll bounce back. I always do," Leigh said, mustering a forced smile.

"Do you think so?" Ron asked, his gaze fixed downward at Leigh, making Leigh feel like a child. Leigh grew impatient. If he were to face the executioner, he preferred to get it over with so he could return home, sleep, and then get to his other home—the real one.

"Listen, Ron, I have to go in there and see Blaireau. I appreciate the pep talk and everything, but I'm gonna be late." A wide smile spread across Ron's face, illuminating it like a giant Christmas tree.

"I suppose. But before you head in, I wanted to let you know that I'm worried about you, Leigh. I've been so for a while now. You don't belong in a place like this, so maybe it's for the best that she's letting you go. But I would have preferred to see you walk away on your own steam. You understand?"

Leigh nodded, and Ron continued, "Something has been going wrong with you for a while. My guess? You've dug yourself into a deep hole with the booze and the drugs. Like the one I just saw you palm," Leigh felt his cheeks flush with heat.

"Take some free advice. You don't have to ride the garbage truck all the way to the dump, know what I mean?" Leigh sobered up slightly. "Goodbye, Leigh," Ron bid him farewell.

Somewhere on the outskirts of his consciousness, Leigh

could hear a woman raising her voice.

CHAPTER 31

"Meeks! Meeks, are you out there?" Blaireau yelled into the hall. Leigh moved toward the voice.

"Enter," Blaireau said, trying to suppress a simmering smile. A sombre expression would be more suitable for the occasion, but she just couldn't help herself. "Sit," she gestured to the chair in front of her desk. For once, the computer appeared to be turned off. *This must be serious business*, Leigh thought, slumping down in the chair with a sigh. The pill was taking effect, and Leigh felt tired.

"Leigh," Blaireau said, brushing a few curls off her forehead. "May I call you Leigh?" A feeble attempt at reassurance.

"No. You may not," Leigh slurred.

Her face flushed with hostility, but just for a moment. He couldn't help admiring how solidly constructed her facade was.

He recalled a day the previous summer when he strolled through his neighbourhood, noticing buildings he had never bothered to look at before. Leigh realized that many of the buildings hid behind a false front, a magician's trick that compelled the eye away from the decaying infrastructure hiding behind it, like capping a rotten tooth.

Most people were like those buildings, he had thought.

They focused their time and money on their street-facing facade, some were nicer than others of course, but the insides remained neglected. Those buildings were rotting from the inside out, infested with rats, and cockroaches that came out at night scuttling over countertops and bedframes. Leaky pipes and mould rotting behind the drywall.

Sitting in Blaireau's office, he saw her like one of those buildings, with the rats, the mould, and the cockroaches crawling around inside her. Eventually, they would consume her.

"They're going to eat you alive," Leigh mumbled.

"I beg your pardon, Mr. Meeks. Didn't quite catch that," she asked.

"THEY'RE GOING TO EAT YOU ALIVE!" Leigh yelled.

Blaireau flinched, then waved away whoever was watching from the hall once she felt safe. Probably Jonesy coming to her rescue (hopefully Ron was still there).

"Mr. Meeks, what I'm about to say might shock you. But I assure you, if you raise your voice to me again, I will have you forcibly removed from the building. Understood?" she warned.

Leigh nodded, perceiving an ugly, jagged crack forming in her facade. Part of him was enjoying this.

"Now, Mr. Meeks, I called you here to inform you that your services will no longer be required at PackUcan. I regret to say that we have to let you go. According to video footage from the warehouse security cameras, it seems you have been sleeping on the job, combined with multiple late sign-ins and coworker complaints about smelling of alcohol. You have left us no choice. Furthermore, as this is a termination, you are not entitled to any severance pay," Blaireau said, sliding an envelope across the desk towards Leigh.

"Inside the envelope, you'll find a check for the hours you accrued during the last pay period and your separation papers and as you are being terminated with cause, I doubt you will be eligible for UI."

Leigh reached for the envelope, never taking his eyes off

her.

"On a personal note, I'm sorry to have to do this, Leigh. I never thought this position was a good fit for you. I genuinely hope you find what you're looking for and wish you the best of luck in your future endeavours," she said, not meaning a word of it.

Leigh blanched, as blood shunted away from the skin on his face. The bubble had finally burst. *Fuckfuckfuck*, but he remained silent, staring down at his hands. Anxiety grabbed him by the throat and started throttling him. Blaireau slid another document and a pen across the desk, asking for his signature. Leigh took the pen, leaned forward, and signed. When he finished, he returned the pen with a shaky hand. Blaireau took the document from him and asked him to stay seated while she made a copy for his records. She whistled as she walked out the door.

At this pivotal moment in Leigh Meeks' downward spiral, one might hope that he would at least give that woman a piece of his mind. Reduce her to a quivering mass. But alas, Leigh Meeks didn't do anything of the sort.

He stumbled out of the office, digging deep in his pocket for the pill that would restore his balance, but there were none there. He knew there should have been at least five pills bouncing around with the lint. On the verge of tears, Leigh teetered down the hallway, passing Ron, who muttered a quiet "Bye Leigh," and headed towards the lobby.

In the dream place, he would have handled things differently. He knew he would have. But in this nightmare, Leigh was weaker than ever, and everything was coming apart quickly. If only he could find one of those damn pills.

Before leaving PackUcan for good, and before she had a chance to photocopy the signed termination letter, he had begged. He begged her for his job. He promised that he would shape up and do better if only she could find it in her heart to give him another chance. He told her he was going to end up on the streets, *for God's sake!* But Blaireau showed him no mercy. She listened politely, but there would be no pardon.

This was a done deal if there ever was one.

An unstoppable force had been set in motion long before his breakdown in her office. Newton's first law of motion states that every object remains at rest or moves in a straight line unless an external force compels it to change, especially if that motion is pointed downhill. Like a ski jump or a car careening down a hill. And once that bastard starts rolling, it's probably best to get out of the way.

Jimmy didn't stand a snowball's chance in hell of getting any sleep that afternoon before his shift. He knew what was coming and he couldn't stop it. Blaireau had called him from home the previous night, letting him know that she would be firing Leigh and advising him to watch out for any last-minute stealing or vandalism in case Leigh somehow caught word.

At the end of his shift Friday morning, Jimmy could barely look Leigh in the face as he checked his bag. He struggled not to give his friend a heads-up so he could prepare himself. But in the end, Jimmy was a company man and couldn't risk losing his job for the sake of friendship, so he remained silent.

Justifying his cowardice, he convinced himself that he would be of no help to Leigh if he was also unemployed. And besides, how would that look on his Police admissions board application? It had been months since his last application, and still nothing. Doing the right thing, he knew, never made anything easier. He considered going to the gym to work off his stress but couldn't find the motivation to get himself out the door. The thought of discussing things with his mother crossed his mind, but he could already hear her response even before the words left her mouth.

"I told you that hoodlum was no good, didn't I? Didn't I tell you?" she would say. "When will you finally listen to your mother and stop making friends with such unsavoury characters? And why on God's green earth do you NEED friends, anyway? You've got me. You have your mother. So, I say, it's a *good thing* he's being let go! Good riddance. I know the type, Jimmy. He would have only led down the garden path and straight into ruin."

No, that would not do at all.

Instead, when she asked him what was bothering him and why he couldn't sleep, knowing he would be tired for his night shift, he simply mentioned his concerns about his police application, that a response should be any day now. Rather than lecture him about applying in the first place, she hit the pantry like a tornado. Amidst the mixing, flipping, frying, and scooping, her only admonishment was, "Jimmy! If you're not going to make a call, put that phone down for the love of Pete."

Back in his room, after burying his conflicting emotions under an avalanche of dopamine-infused butter, sugar, oil, grease, and carbohydrates, Jimmy arranged the dessert around him on the bed, which groaned under his weight. The dessert acted as a safeguard, preventing him from making the wrong decision of calling Leigh to warn him.

He needn't have worried. Four o'clock came and went. The deed was most likely done swiftly. If he knew Blaireau at all, he knew she wasted no time. Sure, she might twist the blade around a bit, as was her style, but she would break it off quick, leaving Leigh to bleed all over the carpet. Jimmy was grateful for small mercies.

Staring at a box of Twinkies, what bothered him the most was his inability to save Leigh. It was a recurring pattern he had noticed, that threaded through the otherwise unpredictable and cruel events of his life. Jimmy had to accept a truth about himself: he had been unable to save anyone.

A first-year psychology student would have told him that his desperate desire to rescue people was the primary motivation behind his application to the police force. They would have also explained that deep down, beneath the sugar-coated synapses of his brain, he believed that by saving the people he loved, he would ultimately save himself. The excuses he had long told himself, were wearing thin.

He had been unable to save his aunt, *but I was only a kid.*

He had been unable to save his dad. *If only I had known what she was doing to him.*

He had been unable to save his friend. *I shouldn't be expected to risk my own job for a friend.*

All reasonable excuses, yet he was no closer to saving himself either.

Fuck that! He had tried to help Leigh at every opportunity. Didn't he lie to Blaireau about Leigh sleeping on the job until she finally asked for the tapes? He had barely dodged that one when she found out. Hadn't he done his best to review Leigh's orders as best he could and re-package his fuck ups? Didn't he express concern and attempt to warn him about the drinking and showing up reeking like a saloon? And didn't he hook him up with his connection, Stan? Didn't he help him get pills when he couldn't sleep? If Leigh was hell-bent on getting himself fired, then be my guest, buddy! Be my guest!

"Jimmy, *KEEP IT DOWN IN THERE!*" His mother yelled. "I don't know who you're talking to, but if you're talking to yourself, don't be surprised if the men in white coats show up and cart you off to the funny farm."

She laughed so hard at this one that it seemed for a minute like she might choke to death right there in James Sr.'s La-Z-Boy recliner. Jimmy decided to wait it out, half-contemplating leaving her there to choke.

Jimmy turned his back on the array of treats that adorned his bedspread - the chocolate eclairs, potato chip bags, chocolate bars, Twinkies, and cans of Coke. He managed to resist them all this time. Unaware of how he had transitioned from the bed to his desk, he found himself with his knees jammed against the wooden drawers. His mother had bought him the desk as a peace offering after his aunt's passing. As he looked down at his hands, he was surprised to see that he had dismantled the gun, placing each piece meticulously in front of him, and preparing to clean it. He had no memory of it at all.

CHAPTER 32

The pills were utterly, positively, fucking gone. Leigh checked and rechecked, checked to make sure and then checked again. He even turned his pockets inside out, meticulously examining deep in the corner folds.

When he burst through the front door of PackUcan, Leigh had his first good look for the pills. Outside, he could finally breathe again, but no amount of breathing eased the crushing anxiety that was bearing down on him. If going completely off the rails was an imminent possibility, he was relieved he hadn't succumbed to his breakdown in front of her. He wouldn't give her the satisfaction.

Leigh emptied his pockets, only to find two dimes and a few clumps of lint. Nothing. If only there had been a nearby public restroom, he would have dashed in and stripped his pants off for a thorough inspection (maybe they fell into the rolled cuffs of his pant legs?).

At the bank, he checked again. No pills. The amount on the cheque was alarmingly low, yet he found solace in the fact that his immediate problem would soon be resolved, allowing him to retreat back to the sanctuary of the dream place. He needed a break.

Approaching the teller, who might have shown concern if

the bank were situated in a more reputable part of the city, Leigh waved the check at her, and she cashed it without raising an eyebrow. Shielded behind the safety of the plexiglass partition, she felt secure. Leigh patted his front pockets a few more times, secured the money, and made a beeline for the gym, hoping to find Stas. It was early, but maybe he'd get lucky.

While waiting for the bus, he couldn't resist another quick pill check. He did the same on the bus until he realized that the woman sitting directly across from him thought he might be vigorously shoving his hands down the front of his pants for a less innocent reason than searching for his medication, so he stopped himself, embarrassed. No pills.

He gave up just as he reached the dilapidated gym with its faded gold facade. Climbing the stairs, he was enveloped in a strong stench of sweat and bleach, that wrapped around him like the humid early summer air. The scent brought comfort. The relief of potentially meeting up with Stas for an exchange washed over him, nearly causing him to wet himself. Praying Stas would be there, he approached the front desk and casually mentioned meeting a friend. In the past, he had relied on Jimmy to get him in with a guest pass, but today he was flying solo.

Spotting Stas, Leigh's excitement got the better of him. He shouted and waved his arms, startled by his reflection in the glass.

"Stas! Hey, Stas!" he called out, but the Russian paid him no attention, engrossed in making advances on a young woman bouncing on a treadmill.

It quickly became apparent to Leigh that showing up unannounced like this was a terrible idea. If it's one thing that drug dealers do not want called to them is *attention*. Realizing Leigh wouldn't leave without a bag, Stas had him buzzed him through, and nearly cut him off right there. It was an empty threat. Leigh was learning that no drug dealer, in the entire history of drug dealing, would turn away a customer with money to spend. NEVER. But the power they hold over customers is as terrifying as it is absolute.

What Leigh failed to recognize was that keeping a customer didn't absolve the dealer from breaking the customer's arm, nose, or collarbone for a transgression like attracting unwanted attention by shouting and wildly waving arms in the middle of a crowded gym.

In the dimly lit stairwell, Stas handed him the pills, demanding a premium for the inconvenience and giving Leigh a warning.

"Next time, maybe I break a finger, yes?" Stas threatened.

"Yes," Leigh replied, handing over the money.

Leigh knew he was treading through a minefield, blindfolded and vulnerable. As he rode the bus home, he struggled to figure out his next move. The best he could come up with was to lay low. Desperate to find solutions, he made absurd promises to himself, hoping they would magically solve all his problems.

Taking the termination letter out of its envelope and flipping it over to the blank side, Leigh removed a pen from his jacket and went to work. He titled it *Promises.* After a moment's thought, he crossed that out and replaced it with *Vows.*

I will only take the pills on weekends.

I will only drink on weekends.

I will find a way to pay off the rent and PAY IT. This is non-negotiable.

On Monday, I will start looking for another night job.

I will eat better.

I will start exercising, but not at Stas' gym.

I will take a break from the dream place.

You will hold your balance no matter what.

By the time Leigh reached the front door of his apartment building, he had discarded the list, tossing it into a nearby garbage can.

The shrill, distorted buzz of the intercom jolted Leigh back. Daylight seeped through the foil in the windows. Did he order takeout? Only food delivery people used the intercom. He felt afraid to answer it. Leigh turned to face the back cushions of the sofa, trying to make himself as small as possible. Maybe they'll go away.

BUZZ. BUZZ.

He covered his ears, taking shallow breaths. The fabric against his nose and forehead grew damp. Silence. *Good*, he thought. Maybe they've gone away. A brief respite enveloped the room, and Leigh was on the verge of sinking back into the dream place when a sudden and jarring pounding on his door jolted him upright. The metallic taste of fear returned to his mouth. Was this it? Were they coming for him? He wondered if they would at least let him sleep wherever they took him. Sleep, after all, was a basic human right, wasn't it? More banging echoed through the apartment. Leigh tossed aside the dirty sheet he had been hiding under, stood up, and hurriedly crossed the living room, accidentally banging his shin on the coffee table with a yelp.

"Damn, *now* they know I'm here," he muttered, his heart racing.

He peered through the peephole. To his astonishment, he recognized the figure standing in the hallway. At that moment, he couldn't discern whether he was still dreaming or truly awake. Since purchasing the drugs from Stas, everything had become very confusing. It was Ron. Goddammit, Ron was standing in the hallway. Seeing him without his overalls was strange, but it was undeniably him. What the hell was he doing here?

"Hey Leigh," Ron called out. "I know you're there. I heard you. Come on, Leigh. Let me in for a second."

Leigh turned the deadbolt and opened the door. Sure enough, there stood Ron, dressed to the nines (well, dressed up for Ron). Leigh stepped aside, allowing Ron to enter. Ron took a thorough look around the apartment, then shifted a few pillows and magazines to one side of the couch before settling himself down.

"How are you, Leigh?" Ron smiled.

He proceeded to explain to Leigh that right after he got fired, he had attempted to track him down. Initially, he tried Blaireau, but that bitch informed him that it was company policy not to disclose employee addresses. Ron thought that was a good one, considering Leigh was no longer an employee, and how could you have a policy about not doing something? Even when he mentioned having a book to return to Leigh, Blaireau still adamantly refused his request.

"Jimmy. Now Jimmy, on the other hand, he's easier. He believes you can use all the friends you can get. It still took a bit of prying to get your address from him, but he eventually caved in, and here I am," Ron said.

"It's good to see you, Ron. You caught me at a bad time. I've been fighting the flu for the past few days and was asleep when you buzzed. Listen, I appreciate you looking in, but maybe we could meet up later, perhaps next week for a coffee or something," Leigh said, remaining near the door.

"Bullshit, Leigh. Looks to me like the only flu you got is the junkie flu," Ron said.

Leigh wasn't accustomed to being called out, and he was growing increasingly uncomfortable, wishing Ron would leave.

"Look, Ron. Thanks for the concern, but I'm fine. I appreciate you making the trip, but you've got it all wrong. With all due respect, you don't have the slightest clue what you're talking about, and I'd like you to leave," Leigh said, his anger rising. All he wanted was for the gentle giant to go.

"Okay, Leigh," Ron said. "Listen to me very carefully now. I have a proposition for you. I didn't come all this way just to be thrown out. So, I'll say my piece, and if you still want me to leave, I'll leave. Fair?"

Leigh thought it over for a moment. His head was pounding, and all he wanted was to lie down, but he liked Ron and didn't want to have to throw him out onto the street, even if he could. His plan was simple: he would listen politely, pretend to consider whatever crazy proposition Ron had in mind, and *then* ask him to leave so that he could return to the dream place.

"Okay, Ron. You win," Leigh said.

"Thanks, Leigh," Ron said, patting the couch cushion beside him, indicating that this might take a while. Leigh took a seat. "I want you to come with me tonight. I won't tell you where; you'll just have to trust me. Can you do that, Leigh?" Leigh remained silent.

"That's what I thought. Let me make it real simple for you. It's no secret that you've been hitting the booze pretty hard lately, and since you've added pills to the mix, you look to me like you might be going down for the count," Ron continued.

"Fucking Jimmy! I knew he couldn't keep his big, fat mouth shut," Leigh muttered.

"Listen, Leigh, Jimmy might be many things, but he isn't a snitch. He thinks you and he are friends, even though you use him. He didn't say anything about the pills," Ron said.

Sensing that time was running out, Ron reached into his wrinkled blazer pocket with his enormous hand and produced a small plastic baggie containing five green pills, tossing them onto the coffee table.

"Where did you get those?" Leigh choked out in disbelief.

"When you and I were talking in Blaireau's hallway, right before she fired you. You nodded off someplace while I was talking, and when you did, I picked your pocket. I saw you pop one pretending to cough. Flu, my ass." Ron said, pressing the index finger of his other hand firmly into the center of Leigh's chest, a reminder not to push him too far.

Leigh sat in stunned silence, his better angels whispering in his ear to hear Ron out.

"So here it is. I'll make it easy for you. You come with me for a couple of hours tonight, and then I'll give you back these five little green wheels that take you nowhere," Ron paused, leaning closer to Leigh on the couch until they were eye to eye, and simply said, "And if you don't, then I might just have to carry you out of here kicking and screaming. Don't think I won't do it. And just to be safe, I'll find every last pill you've got and flush them down the fucking toilet. Got me?"

"I'll get my things."

CHAPTER 33

I'm at a Tim Hortons. Barely made it out of there in one piece. And that fucker lied to me. He promised to return my pills but he didn't. I thought he was taking me to some church group sing-song (he looks the type) or maybe out to grab a bite.

Instead, he took me to an NA meeting, if you can believe that! Me, at a fucking Narcotics Anonymous meeting, can you imagine? He told me this sob story about his high school days, how he got tangled up with the wrong crowd and started using crystal meth and that his daddy didn't love him, and with God's help, he got sober a few years ago.

He called himself a grateful addict. All I heard was "grateful this" and "grateful that." I wanted to puke. And the people there. It was like a cult. Ron sat me down in the front row of this church basement, yanking me up when it was time to stand and pulling me down to sit. It's worse than the Catholics.

At the bottom of the stairs going in, there were people shaking hands, like degenerate Walmart greeters, all smiles, of course.

"Hey Leigh, welcome."
"Hi Leigh, I'm Cindy. You're in the right place."

"Hello Leigh, you are no longer alone."

I shook some hands and mumbled a few hellos, but I couldn't help feeling embarrassed for them. Then the meeting started, and they launched right into this God stuff, which I found really offensive. This guy rambled on about how fucked up he had been on cocaine, all the horrible things he did to people, and now with the help of God and his sponsor, everything is rosy. What a fucking moron!

I would have got up and walked on the spot if Ron hadn't blackmailed me with my own PROPERTY! Those pills are MINE!!! If he truly understood what I'm going through, he would've given them back and left me alone. What Ron fails to grasp is that I'm not an addict. I only take the pills, and drink, for that matter to help me sleep. And as I've explained, when I sleep, I escape to a dream place where everything is better than it is here. If Ron knew all that, maybe he would take the fucking pills too, but he never gave me a chance to explain. He just kept on about his problems and how fantastic things are since he got sober.

Fantastic? Well, if it's so fantastic, why is he working nights at some shit job breaking down cardboard? If that's his version of fantastic, then he can have it. I'll take the dream place any day of the week. Besides, I can stop whenever I want to.

Had to pause there for a minute. I'm sitting at a Tim Hortons downtown, having a coffee before heading back to the apartment, just trying to decompress after that shitshow and the manager came over and threatened to kick me out if I didn't keep the noise down. Keep the noise down? I'm writing a fucking letter. So, I set him straight on a few things, and I think he'll leave me alone now. He claimed I was yelling. Yelling! Can you believe that?

Where was I? Right, the meeting. Another guy stood up and started interpreting what they call the slogans, which are basically a bunch of platitudes and clichés meant for four-year-olds. I wasn't sure how much more I could handle, but I'd had a rough day and needed those damn pills, so I listened. This guy stood at the microphone preaching about ONE

DAY AT A TIME, BUT FOR THE GRACE OF GOD, and YOU ARE NO LONGER ALONE, the one I heard on the way in. Fuck do these guys repeat themselves. I got it, okay? Let's move on. After a few announcements (where you could smoke etc.), they moved on to the CHIPS.

So, this other guy gets up and takes his sweet ass time walking up to the mic like he was on his way to collect an Academy Award or something and believe me it's nothing like that. I know what it's like to get an award. I've written books that have won awards. Anyway, he went on about how the chips were important in his sobriety journey, blah blah, and then he began the countdown.

"Does anyone have nine months of continuous sobriety? No takers?"
Then the cult responds in unison, "Keep coming back," another golden oldie from the collection of slogans.

"Anyone with six months?"
"Keep coming back."

On and on this goes until he gets down to the last chip and I should have guessed.

"And now, the most important chip. The desire chip. Is there anyone here tonight with a desire to stop using, just for today?"

And of course, the whole room was looking at me. I could feel my face flushing and all I could do was to look down at the tops of my shoes. Ron even nudged me, but I didn't move. Fuck them. They weren't going to get me up there. Then the guy said, "If it's your first time here and you're too uncomfortable to come up, see me after the meeting, and I'll make sure you get a chip. Thanks all. Enjoy your meeting."

I almost stood up and left right then and there, but with all eyes on me, I figured it might be better to stay put a little longer. I felt somewhat relieved when they introduced the speaker. Anything to shift the focus away from me.

So, then this woman took the stage and started talking about her perfect childhood. Not a drop of alcohol in her family, no drugs or pills, not even a beer at a Sunday barbecue or a glass of wine with dinner. Her parents were loving, kind, and supportive, married for fifty-one years until her father passed away in his sleep. In high school, she got drunk a few times before dances, just like all her friends. She got married, had a successful career in real estate, had a couple of kids, and by the end of her story, she lost everything. Right down the crapper. And you know how? Pills. A genuine addict, the genuine article.

At that moment, I realized the whole thing had been a setup. A carefully orchestrated plan to reel me in. Fresh blood for the cult. It was painfully obvious. She had been staring directly at me the entire time. I suppose they expected me to break down or have some kind of breakthrough. Boy, did they pick the wrong guy.

I left during the applause, walking straight down the center aisle, up the stairs, and back onto the street. I fully expected Ron to follow, but thankfully he didn't. I suppose he could see that his plan had failed.

That manager keeps looking over at me from behind the counter. He's been talking to another employee, but I'm too far away to hear their conversation. Even though I'm not carrying any pills, it's probably best not to stick around here. Besides, it's late, and I'm exhausted. I think I'll head back to my apartment and try to figure out my next move. It's been one hell of a day, and I just need to be alone for a while and regroup.

Love,
Leigh

CHAPTER 34

Summoning courage, Leigh walked through the front door of his apartment building, exerting every ounce of willpower he had left. Before climbing the stairs to his apartment, Leigh checked the time: 10:34 PM. He hoped the Superintendent had the television turned up loud as usual, allowing him to slip into his apartment unnoticed. At least Stas had been at the gym, making sure Leigh had enough to keep him going for a while. And when he ran out again? He would jump off that bridge when he got to it. Besides, he was *certain* he'd have another job by then. He'd get right on that and make things right. Passing his mailbox, he made a promise to check it tomorrow. Had he bothered to look, he would have been better prepared for what was to come.

Approaching his unit, Leigh noticed something stuck to his door beside the handle - a yellow flyer or maybe a "do not disturb" notice like the ones found on hotel doors. Blaireau and Jonesy had one hanging on their motel room door as Leigh transitioned from a stagger to a scamper.

Eviction. By order of the sheriff's office.

Dizziness and nausea washed over Leigh as he tried the key in the lock. It wouldn't turn. He tried again, shaking it around, but nothing happened. The yellow paper mentioned calling a number to arrange a time to collect his possessions, warning that failing to make the call would result in the seizure and auction of his belongings. It had finally happened, and Leigh vomited the meagre contents of his stomach all over the hallway carpet.

Leigh ran through the empty streets, his heart pounding, until he couldn't run anymore. Seeking cover in a sparsely wooded park, he huddled beside the trunk of an ancient maple tree, wrapping his arms around his knees and rocking. Leigh prayed for help. None came.

"Hey Jimbo," Crystal said.

"What's up?"

"Call for you in the shack," she replied.

Jimmy had a few hours left on his shift. Who the hell could be calling at this hour? He hoped it wasn't Blaireau - he'd had enough of her for one day. Knowing his mother would be asleep, and it being too early for anyone else, he unlocked the door to the security office, set down the Twinkie he was eating, and lifted the receiver.

"PackUcan, security. You're speaking to Jimmy," he said.

"Jimmy! Thank God. It's Leigh."

"Leigh, how are you doing? You hanging in there?" Jimmy asked.

"Jimmy, listen. I'm in trouble. I need your help," Leigh said. "I've been kicked out. They evicted me. Changed the locks at my place. I've been wandering around, trying to figure out what to do. I need your help, Jimmy. Please. I have nowhere to go," Leigh pleaded, tracing his finger along the buttons of the payphone.

"Where are you now?" he asked in full cop mode.

"I don't know! Wait, there's a sign. Hang on. I'm in Viewmount Park," Leigh replied.

"Okay, Leigh, listen to me very carefully," Jimmy said. "Can you get yourself to my place? I should be there in about three hours. You'll have to kill some time until then, but it's the best

I can do."

"I think so. I'll walk it," Leigh replied.

"Okay, that's good. My mother will be home but don't worry, I'll handle her. But Leigh?" Jimmy heard Leigh's breathing beginning to slow down. "I think you should consider going to your landlord and see about your things."

"No, Jimmy. I just can't right now. I'm tired. I can't face it. I've been throwing up, and I just need a place to get my head together. Can you do that for me, Jimmy?" Jimmy thought for a moment.

"Okay, don't worry, man," Jimmy said. "Take a minute and pull yourself together, and I'll see you at my place," Jimmy repeated the address three times to make sure Leigh got it.

"And Jimmy?" Leigh said.

"Yeah, Leigh?"

"Thank you," Leigh said and ended the call.

How could I have been so stupid, Leigh thought. *Don't beat yourself up, it was Ron's fault. If he hadn't stolen from me, I wouldn't be in this mess. Listen, the reason doesn't matter. It was careless and stupid. Besides, it doesn't change a thing.*

I can't sleep. It has been 5 days. I can't sleep. The inner dialogue had started shortly after arriving at Jimmy's and continued incessantly since then. Leigh supposed it was understandable given the extreme circumstances. Forgetting his wallet or money at the apartment were forgivable oversights. But the pills? How could he have been so careless?

Leigh felt grateful to be staying at Jimmy's house. However, it was evident right from the get-go that Jimmy's mother did not want him there. Leigh had to give credit to his friend for putting up a pretty good fight on his behalf, and after some back and forth, she finally relented. It was when Jimmy played the Love Thy Neighbor card that she threw her hands up and relented, but only with strict conditions.

Leigh breathed a sigh of relief when Jimmy won her over, but he still winced at the Love Thy Neighbor speech. Standing on the threshold before being allowed inside, Leigh listened to her demands: He could stay for a maximum of two weeks or until he found another place to live, whichever came first. No girls. No alcohol or drugs on or off the premises. He would be expected to contribute to the cleaning. THE KITCHEN WAS OFF-LIMITS. He would search for a job and he could borrow some of Jimmy's clothes until he could retrieve his belongings or buy new ones.

After agreeing to her lengthy list, Jimmy showed Leigh to the guest room and left him alone to settle in. Leigh quietly closed the door and wept.

Jimmy and Leigh spent the afternoon talking things over. Initially, Leigh couldn't comprehend why Jimmy's mom had buckled during the Love Thy Neighbor speech. She didn't strike him as much of a believer. However, when Jimmy showed him his bedroom, Leigh understood, and in that flash of understanding, he remembered the Christmas card Jimmy had given him. *Jimmy was a believer.*

What had started as a childhood hobby akin to stamp collecting had transformed into a disturbing fanaticism that made Leigh uneasy. He thought about the gun Jimmy had shown him. Fanaticism and firearms were a dangerous combination. So much for sanctuaries. She should have included law enforcement in that list, Leigh thought to himself. "If, by any chance, the police raid the premises in search of the Jesus freak with the gun, our generous hospitality will be revoked, and you'll be promptly kicked out, mister."

Jimmy and Leigh sat on Jimmy's bed, discussing what Leigh's next steps should be. Leigh believed paying a visit to Stas at the gym was the right move, while Jimmy suggested contacting the Superintendent. They went back and forth on the matter, pausing briefly when Jimmy's mother entered the room, carrying a tray of frosty root beer floats, which she placed on Jimmy's desk alongside his collection of Jesus bobbleheads. Leigh threatened to leave if Jimmy kept pushing, and in turn, Jimmy threatened him with his mother if he tried to score more pills from Stas. An impasse was reached.

This stalemate had endured for a full five days, with Leigh's suffering failing to budge Jimmy from his position. Thoughts of his aunt, suffering in a hospital bed due to alcohol and God knows what else, consumed Jimmy. He was determined not to let the same thing happen to Leigh. He would nurse him through the withdrawal process, and that's exactly what he did.

Initially, Leigh showed no signs of improvement. Even after five days, he had yet to sleep a wink. He had read somewhere that the record was eleven days. Some teenager in the 1960s had managed it. Once or twice during Leigh's intense drug-sick begging, Jimmy almost succumbed and considered visiting Stas himself. However, he knew that anything he obtained for Leigh would only provide temporary relief. It was better to rip off the band-aid all at once. Pull it off clean.

Early on in the first evening, Leigh's condition deteriorated rapidly. His hands trembled, his mood grew dark and savage, and he repeatedly asked if they could go to the gym together, maybe Jimmy could lend him some money to get a few more pills just to taper off with. Jimmy had no idea what to expect from drug withdrawal, but he would be damned if he was going to leave Leigh alone with his mother. He decided to take a couple of unused vacation days, even though it pissed Blaireau off, due to the last-minute request. However, considering the multitude of balls she was juggling, losing a less-than-satisfactory yet conscientious and loyal security guard was something she wasn't prepared to deal with at the moment.

The withdrawal began with what seemed like a severe bout of the flu. Leigh did his best to tolerate the muscle aches and cramps. At times, he appeared disoriented and never slept. However, the flu quickly progressed into a combination of watery loose stools, vomiting, blurred vision, and a total loss of appetite.

Late on Wednesday night, well after Jimmy's mother had turned in, Leigh started babbling about needing to get back to his other life, incessantly repeating the name Charlotte. Jimmy had never heard Leigh mention a Charlotte before. Leigh shouted for his grandmother, pleading with her to keep Ms. Hewitt away from him. He begged to see Stas and implored Jimmy to get him more pills, promising he would do *anything*. In a moment of weakness, when Leigh groaned that he would agree to meet his landlord, Jimmy almost gave in. *Maybe one pill would be okay.*

Leigh's delirium snapped Jimmy back to his senses. Leigh explained to Jimmy that he couldn't reach the place without sleep. Sleep was the gateway, the portal, the door to that realm. Sleep was God, Heaven, and Jesus all rolled into one. It was this kind of talk that got Jimmy *scared*. Leigh was in real trouble, and Jimmy feared one of three things might happen: Leigh could die from a convulsion or seizure, he could find his gun and demand relief, or spiral into the abyss and never return. Bye-bye, Leigh. Nice knowing ya.

Leigh shit the bed, and Jimmy took care of cleaning it up. After the first time, Jimmy made a special trip to the new Walmart to purchase a set of plastic sheets, the kind commonly used for toddlers or the elderly. Despite Jimmy's efforts to get rid of the reek with copious amounts of air freshener and windows wide open, the room still carried the faint smell of shit, vomit, and disinfectant.

In the end, Leigh did not go insane or take his own life (praise Jesus). By the fourth day, things started to improve. Leigh managed to keep down some of the food prepared by Jimmy's mother. Even the mother seemed to be displaying some compassion toward Leigh, an emotion Jimmy had believed her incapable of. Perhaps she simply enjoyed the fact that Leigh was helpless, or maybe the Holy Spirit had touched her and saved her soul. Whatever the reason, Jimmy felt relieved not to have to fight a battle on two fronts.

By that afternoon, colour returned to Leigh's cheeks, and his eyes no longer appeared sunken like a mouse peeking out of its hole. After Jimmy personally prepared a bowl of chicken soup with crushed square salted crackers sprinkled on top, he asked Leigh if he felt he would be okay staying with his mom, as he should probably be getting back to work.

Leigh nodded, grinning at his caretaker. Leigh still hadn't slept, but he no longer cared.

CHAPTER 35

The phone rang as Jimmy inspected his security uniform spread out on the bed, recalling his late father's admonition about keeping collars and cuffs clean. No matter how hard he scrubbed, the light brown rings remained. The stains embarrassed him.

"I'll get it," he said.

"You get it, Jimmy. My stories are on," they said over each other. On the way to the kitchen, Jimmy made sure to close Leigh's door. He lifted the receiver off the kitchen wall, the cord hung low like a noose.

"Hello," Jimmy said.

"Good afternoon, James." It was Blaireau, and her voice sounded happy.

"Good afternoon," Jimmy replied.

"Jimmy, who is it?" His mother called from the living room. Covering the mouthpiece, he shouted back, "It's work!"

"Tell them you'll be right in. You've taken too much time off."

"Have I caught you at a bad time?" Blaireau asked.

"No. It's fine. Just my mother," Jimmy said. "I was actually just about to call you."

"I see. Listen, I don't make a habit of calling employees on their days off, but this is important. It's an emergency," she said.

"An emergency? Is everything all right? Has anyone been hurt?"

"No, nothing like that. But I need to ask you, have you been in contact with Ranleigh Meeks?"

"Why? What's wrong?" Jimmy asked.

"This is strictly confidential. Can I trust you with something?" Blaireau knew which buttons to push. "Of course," Jimmy replied, plucking a chocolate doughnut from a cardboard box on the kitchen table while waiting for her response.

"The police have been here. They are trying to locate Mr. Meeks. They want to ask him a few questions and have been unable to find him. You don't have any idea where they could find him, do you?"

"No, I don't," he lied. He no longer felt like eating and returned the doughnut to the box, closing the lid.

"I see," she said, sounding disappointed.

"Is he in trouble or something?"

"I'd say so, James. Hate to cut your vacation short, but I'm wondering if you might be able to come in for your shift tonight," Blaireau said.

"I was planning to have a late dinner with my mother, but if you think it's absolutely necessary," Jimmy laid it on thick, feeling guilty. *Jesus forgive me*, he thought.

"I think it would be best," she said. "If you could make it in an hour or so early, we can discuss this further."

"Um, sure, okay," Jimmy said. "Do you know why they're looking for him? The police, I mean."

"If you can keep this under your hat. They seem to think he's involved with drugs."

"What? That's impossible. That doesn't sound like something he'd ever do," Jimmy replied.

Blaireau continued, "Be that as it may, they are looking for him, and they will most likely arrest him if they find him. He has been evicted from his apartment. The rental agency contacted the police after finding baggies of illegally obtained opiates. They've been to his apartment, and it's a complete mess. It looks like our friend Mr. Meeks has been living a double life," her serious tone barely masked the glee that threatened to rush up in her like a geyser. When she said *double life*, the words hit Jimmy hard. *My other life*, wasn't that what Leigh said? "Jimmy, are you there?"

"Yes, sorry. I'm here."

"Anyway, they didn't find much, but they found a stack of letters he had sent piled up in his mailbox - return to sender. The police had a look at them, and they think they were written by someone struggling with schizophrenia. I'm in them, Phyllis at reception, and Jerry Jones from sales, and Ron. They wouldn't give me any more details as it's an active investigation. Anyway, I've said too much. I'll see you soon?"

"Yes, Ma'am," Jimmy responded.

"And Jimmy," she didn't wait for a response, "If you hear from him, try to find out where he is and let me know immediately." The line went dead.

"Hey, Jim," a voice behind him said. Jimmy screamed and dropped the phone on the kitchen floor with a crack. Leigh was standing in the front hall. "Sorry, man, I didn't mean to startle you, is everything alright?"

Withdrawal from the pills and alcohol had been a nightmare. Leigh kept praying for sleep, but it never came. Why couldn't he sleep? Every single minute he was painfully aware of his sickness. He had to lie there while Jimmy cleaned up his shit and puke. At first, even water made him vomit. Every cell in his body felt cancerous. He begged Jimmy to get him more pills, but Jimmy was a dedicated jailer. He had even stopped going to work to keep an eye on him.

In the last twelve hours, Leigh hallucinated with eyes wide open, seeing Jimmy as a giant, attempting to poke a finger or two through the wire cage surrounding Leigh's bed. The trap.

He felt his body roll backward and forward as he convulsed. In his hallucination, he crouched behind a bright red hamster wheel while Jimmy played with him. Jimmy's breath clouded the air with the smell of doughnuts and instant coffee. Leigh did his best to make the giant go away and leave him alone. He squeezed his eyes shut and slapped his hands over his ears, but the giant would not leave him alone.

From under the bed covers Leigh heard Jimmy on the phone. The person on the other end had a lot to say. Jimmy's answers did nothing to reveal the nature of the call, but Leigh had a terrible feeling. An alarm went off in his head. Leigh felt a sudden urge to get to his feet.

Wrapping the duvet around his emaciated frame, he managed to make his way down the stairs to the main hall of the house, just outside the kitchen. He rounded the staircase as Jimmy was finishing his call. Leaning on the banister for support, he called out to Jimmy and startled him.

Jimmy seemed nervous, and that wasn't good. He helped Leigh the rest of the way to the kitchen and offered him a doughnut, which Leigh accepted.

It looked like Jimmy was heading back to PackUcan, which on its own wouldn't have caused any alarm, but Jimmy hadn't *made* the call. Somebody from work, probably Blaireau, had called him, and their conversation made him jumpy. Leigh asked if everything was all right, and Jimmy told him that his replacement called in sick, so they needed him to cover.

Jimmy was a terrible liar.

Looking out of the guestroom window, Leigh realized that he needed to leave Jimmy's place as soon as he could. Although the worst of the withdrawal seemed to be behind him, the fact that he had gone days without sleep concerned him. In his utter exhaustion, everything moved at a slower pace. It felt as if he was navigating the bottom of a fish tank, reminiscent of aquarium ornaments like the deep-sea diver. He felt very much like that deep-sea diver, with his leg raised mid-step, clinging to life by the thinnest of breathing tubes. One thing was clear: he had to get out of Jimmy's place.

After his chat with Jimmy hovering over the box of doughnuts, Leigh retreated to the guest room to think things over. Fixated on the ancient dresser at the foot of the bed, Leigh was torn between two prevailing thoughts: What am I going to do for money, and did that lunatic Blaireau call the police? He hadn't arrived at any conclusions yet. In the end, he succumbed to paranoia.

The police were on the lookout for him, and they had discovered his stash. His landlord would likely be the first to know, followed by his workplace. Despite Jimmy's attempts to appear like a tough guy, Leigh knew that he was as soft as the gooey filling inside one of his jelly doughnuts. If anyone from the police department talked to Jimmy for more than three minutes, he would give him up just like that. It wouldn't be long before the police came knocking on the door.

Leigh's choice, though challenging, was straightforward. So, what do we have behind door number one? HOMELESSNESS. And door number two? POSSESSION OF A CONTROLLED SUBSTANCE FOR THE PURPOSE OF TRAFFICKING – MINIMUM 2 YEARS IN PRISON.

Leigh would take his chances on the street. He would not survive in jail. This all sounded good in his head, but Leigh was frail, had never lived on the street and had no money. It would be straight from the relative comfort of Jimmy's, right to the streets. Just like his transition from here to the dream place, but in this case, instead of from bearable to paradise; it would be from shitty to shittier. If only he could sleep on it.

Somewhere in the fog of his mind, he sensed the beginnings of an idea, somewhere back there taking shape behind his eyes. Beginning life as a tiny seed, breaking open and starting its ascent. Soon, it would reveal itself to Leigh, and he would be grateful.

Rooting through the room had taken longer than he had anticipated. His hands shook and he was moving slow. But he had found what he was looking for. The Jesus figurines made him uncomfortable, this was stealing after all, but on balance, when all the credits and debits were finally added up, he felt he would be forgiven given the circumstances.

The desk drawers in Jimmy's room were well-stocked with candy bars and bags of potato chips. Startled, he jumped when a mummified face on the cover of a book he found in the first drawer stared back at him. Its eye sockets rotted, on the verge of crumbling to dust. Four dirty, protruding teeth hovered above a soft, feminine chin. The neck was thin, like somebody with enormous hands had squeezed the life out of the boy. Leigh closed the drawer. The second drawer was locked. He had found what he was looking for. Might have to jimmy this open, he thought, suppressing a giggle that threatened to turn to a shriek. Jimmy, that was a good one.

After a few attempts, the lock finally gave way, almost knocking a model of Noah's Ark off the desktop. It was a child's lock. He pulled the drawer open, accompanied by a dull thud, and a scraping against the plywood. Jackpot.

When he had finished gathering his newly acquired necessities, Leigh crept back to the guest room careful not to draw any attention from Jimmy's mother. He needed to sit and rest. Of course, sleeping was out of the question, so he settled onto a plastic-covered chair beside the ancient dresser before heading out the door for good.

CHAPTER 36

Leigh's legs, weary and battered by the relentless march from Jimmy's house, finally gave up the ghost and surrendered to a table in the narrow expanse of the Cumberland Terrace food court. Leigh was an experienced shopping mall wayfarer. He had wasted a good many hours he might have otherwise been productive wandering giant hallways and dining in food courts. There was something safe about a shopping mall for Leigh. It was a place he couldn't be found.

Cumberland Terrace is an odd place, a relic of the seventies when concrete monstrosities were the architectural norm. The upper floor was practically deserted, save for the odd caretaker who still cared enough to water the plants that continued to flourish in large wooden planters permanently situated between the long wooden benches that overlooked Cumberland Avenue.

Buried deep in the basement just beyond the rumbling and screeching trains of Bay subway station, the food court itself was spread out like an elongated bowling alley, a twisted caricature of what it once was, its vibrance long since replaced by the cold, sterile glow of worn-out fluorescent lighting. Food kiosks lined up where the gutters should have been, forgotten enterprises that failed to keep up with the times, like an '80s hangover. A pizza joint, a bagel place, chicken teriyaki and mall sushi. The city had often hinted at a full demolition to make way for new condo towers and a modern shopping experience but had yet to make good on that promise.

The metal tables, scattered and abandoned, were testimony to an era of hustle and bustle that had long since retreated. If you squinted just right, you could almost see the spectral figures of weekend shoppers huddled over their trays of food court fare. But the tables now were deserted. It was late. At best, Leigh had seen four, maybe five souls wander in here. He felt their eyes on him.

Leigh was still able to pass as one of them. The stolen oversized hoodie and the gym bag from Jimmy's still gave him the air of a midnight rambler rather than a man on the cusp of homelessness. But he knew in his gut that this was a disguise that wouldn't last. There was a strange sense of safety in this anonymity.

Leigh hoisted the stolen gym bag over his shoulder and dragged himself one more time through the halls of the Cumberland Terrace, like a spirit unwilling to leave the world of the living. But the mall eventually spat him out onto Yonge Street, across from the Toronto Reference Library. Out there, without the lonesome comfort of the mall's shelter, he was exposed and ready.

CHAPTER 37

3 AM would normally signify the middle of the afternoon for Leigh Meeks, but afternoons had ceased to exist. His life had evolved into one long day, measured solely by light and dark. It was similar to walking into a room and flicking the light switch on and off again. Holding onto his energy would have been one thing, but he couldn't shake the feeling that he had become like a clock that was slowly winding down.

The dumpster was parked directly below a large rectangular sign. The sign, white lettering on a purple background, read: "Totally Nude Female Interactive Dancing." The back alley had been designed to serve two purposes for the businesses that backed onto it: a quasi-parking lot for high-rolling customers, and an area with enough cover to conceal midnight sexual favours and drug deals. Two female dancers perched high on a fire escape, dressed in lifeguard-red swimsuits that were cut high over their hips. Leigh thought to himself, *must be Baywatch night at the old strip club*. He had considered going in but had no money and couldn't risk his bag being searched by the bouncer.

A steel door from the neighbouring building swung open. The women finished the joint they were sharing and returned to the club. Leigh had expected a busboy to emerge from the door, although he wasn't sure why. It just seemed like the kind of door a busboy might use.

Sitting behind the dumpster, Leigh tried to make himself as small as possible in case someone was taking out the trash. Life, Leigh thought, existed in those moments that fell between the immovable slabs of experiences, like cracks in the sidewalk. Cigarette breaks, tediously overcrowded subway rides to work, traffic jams where people got worked up listening to talk radio, lunchtimes, once-a-year southern vacations, a few puffs of a joint on a fire escape, or a quick smoke break beside a dumpster, reeking of someone else's discarded dinner. That was where people revealed themselves. While lost in this thought, he heard voices speaking in Russian, laughing.

Leigh would later recall the events that followed in fragments like a long strip of film cut randomly with some pieces removed and then the film taped back together. His breathing grew faster and shallower as he listened to their conversation and quietly got himself into a crouched position.

With clenched teeth, he slowly unzipped the gym bag and pulled out the gun, ensuring that the safety was off. He would remember thinking that if he didn't act right then, they would return inside, and he would have blown it. Leigh wouldn't recall getting to his feet or approaching the men from behind the dumpster, pistol in hand. Nor would he remember what he initially said to them. However, he did remember standing about six feet away from Stas and the bodyguard, his raised hand trembling violently under the weight of the gun.

Both men had their hands in the air, like on TV. Leigh was so frightened that he thought he might wet his pants. He felt neither the urge to fight nor to run. He felt stuck. He felt like bowing his head to them, surrendering, groveling—anything so they wouldn't hurt him.

"Come on, Leigh. You want this? This will be very bad for you," Stas said to him. "Why don't you come upstairs, and we talk," his accent thicker than Leigh had ever heard it.

Leigh's hand shook so badly that he worried he might drop the gun or accidentally shoot Stas or his buddy in the face, but lowering the weapon was out of the question.

"Just the baggie in your sock. Just give that over, and I'm outta here," Leigh said.

Stas' face went blank, like a slab of marble waiting to be carved into some expression. He muttered something to the bodyguard in Russian out of the side of his mouth.

"Okay, Leigh," he said, sticking his chest out in a Superman pose and lowering his hands to his waist. "You come and take. Come and take from me, or shoot me," appearing decidedly more in control of the situation than Leigh was.

At that moment, everything happened, like a race after the starter gun goes off. A woman screamed from above him, another dancer crouched on the fire escape. "Stas! Watch it, Stas! He has a gun!"

The bodyguard made his play, surprising Leigh with his speed despite his size. The knife was angled outward and away from his body. If Leigh hadn't looked back when he did, the knife would have pierced through his left rib cage and into his lung, effectively ending his campaign to rob Stanislav and probably his life.

When he saw the knife swing toward him, the full tilt of primal, monkey adrenaline fired on all cylinders. Leigh's amygdala, the part of his brain responsible for alerting extreme danger, sent a signal to the command center, the hypothalamus, triggering the flood of adrenaline. All within fractions of a second, the command center ordered the adrenal nukes to fire. The silos were now empty, and Leigh moved fast.

He squeezed the trigger, moving to the right and away from the man with the knife. There was more screaming, from above and below. The man dropped the knife and fell to the ground. Blood sprayed from where his big toe had been just seconds earlier. Momentarily distracted by the sheer volume of blood, Leigh briefly took his eyes off Stas. Now it was Stanislav's turn, and as he made his move, another Baywatch lifeguard screamed, "Watch out!" Leigh's head swiveled back towards the bulky figure charging at him. Leigh instinctively aimed the gun's muzzle at the Russian, his hand still trembling. This sudden action stopped Stas dead in his tracks. Leigh could hear sirens approaching in the distance. He thought of Verna Hewitt.

"Stas! Come on. The bag," Leigh spluttered. "Before I shoot you, too," he shrugged as if the gun wasn't fully under his control. Stas remained focused on the wobbly gun, now worried that it might go off again. He lowered a hand to his ankle, retrieved the plastic bag, and tossed it at Leigh's feet.

"We go now, yes?" Stas gestured toward the approaching sirens.

"The money too," Leigh croaked.

"You take drugs, I keep money. Deal?"

"No, Stas, fuck you, no deal," Leigh screamed. "Give me the money."

Without money, he wouldn't get far. One final push, and then he could rest. He could sleep. The sirens grew nearer, and with a gunshot fired, the police would be armed and ready to rock 'n' roll.

Leigh's perception distorted everything he heard and saw. Everything came to a halt. His mind played an association game, a final attempt to keep the organism called Leigh sane. With a desperate grasp at straws, Leigh's mind conjured an image of a Roman slave in an arena and Stas a Gladiator who, given the chance, would decapitate Leigh without a second thought. More dancers gathered on the fire escape, resembling Roman nobility with faces powdered white with arsenic. It was this revelation of his slavery that sent his fear packing.

The deck had always been stacked against him and always would be. Memories of childhood bullies, the Blaireaus of the world, the system that relied on him but never rewarded him—caused a rage that consumed him. And suddenly, Leigh found himself back in the parking lot behind a strip club. This was the last stop.

Leigh raised the gun and pointed it directly at Stanislav's face, taking three steps toward him and speaking with a tone of voice that had never before issued from his mouth, "THE

MONEY."

A change came over Stas. The confidence leaked from his overdeveloped, steroid-injected muscles. Leigh watched him literally deflate. With cocksureness replaced by fear for his life, Stas bent before Leigh, fumbled with the money roll hidden in his other sock, and held it out to be taken.

"Stand up," Leigh commanded.

The Russian obeyed, and as he straightened himself to a fully upright position, Leigh brought the butt of the gun down hard on the bridge of Stas' nose. The slave was free.

PART FIVE

COMA

CHAPTER 38

Toronto General Hospital. Leigh received a grade of 3 on the Glasgow Coma Scale, which rates a patient's level of consciousness on a scale of 3 to 15. Originally published in 1974 by Graham Teasdale and Bryan J. Jennett, professors of neurosurgery at the University of Glasgow, the scale aims to assess a patient's state of consciousness. The scale consists of three tests: eye, verbal, and motor.

For instance, if a patient does not open their eyes, they score one point. Opening their eyes in response to a voice results in three points. Similar grading applies to the verbal and motor portions of the test. In short, if a patient fails to open their eyes, make any sound, or exhibit any movement, they receive an overall score of three points (one point per category). A score of three represents the worst possible outcome on the test. Leigh's score was a solid three.

Leigh had been in a coma for a full five days, leaving the doctors at a complete loss. His coma was not medically induced to reduce the risk of brain injury from physical trauma, meningitis, or rabies. He arrived at the hospital early in the morning via ambulance, showing no obvious signs of trauma. The attending physician ruled out traumatic head injury, ordering a complete blood count. Stroke was the next potential cause on the doctor's list, although the patient was too young for that. Brain tumour, infection, or drug/alcohol intoxication followed as possible causes. If the doctor were a betting man, he would have wagered on drugs. He would have lost that bet.

In the days following Leigh's arrival, he had become somewhat of a medical marvel and local hospital celebrity. The bloodwork and CAT scan turned up no explanations for his sudden coma. Leigh's case became a wait-and-see situation. If he showed no signs of improvement, they would have to consider transferring him to a long-term healthcare facility, as they needed the bed. While discussing the potential transfer with a hospital administrator, the doctor's pager vibrated in his pocket.

The patient was awake.

Leigh attempted to open his eyes but found them glued shut. He perceived his throat as a cylinder of sandpaper, making swallowing nearly impossible. The pain seemed to radiate to the fillings in his mouth. He felt intense thirst and in need of water but believed he had lost any voice with which to ask. In the darkness, he couldn't be sure if anyone was there to hear him. Leigh decided to stay still. Perhaps he could go back to... sleep? It hadn't been sleeping exactly; he wasn't certain what it had been. He could hear soft, rhythmic beeps from a machine monitoring his vital signs, but without the ability to see, he could only assume he was in a hospital bed.

His memory had become unreliable. Even *if* he could recall everything, he would have to admit to being profoundly confused lately. Hospital bed. Did Stas come after him after Leigh shattered his nose in God knows how many places? Despite his missing toe, did Leon, the bodyguard rise and lunge at him, finally landing the knife where he had originally intended it to go? Was Leigh too slow in leaving the scene, resulting in a shootout with the police? He simply couldn't remember.

Everything immediately after breaking Stas' nose was a

complete and utter blank. However, there was something peaceful about being in this room. A tranquillity found in a forced surrender. Leigh supposed it didn't matter whether it was Stas, Leon, or the police who had put him here. The jig was up, and with that came a sense of relief. Another peculiar thing was that Leigh felt physically fine. No pain anywhere. Just thirst and a headache. Even the torment of withdrawal from alcohol and Oxys had apparently ceased. Maybe he had been here much longer than he first thought.

An intention prompted his brain to signal his hand to move toward his face, to see if he could touch his eyes and unglue them. Stuck. Halted. Restrained. Blocked. Trapped. The words came all at once. So, it was the police who had apprehended him after all. His wrists were in restraints and it was over. Leigh was now sure the police had nabbed him in the alley after robbing Stas. His next stop would be jail. Opening his eyes no longer seemed necessary. Maybe if he just lay there quietly, they might forget all about him. Wouldn't that be nice?

The patient had moved his head from side to side and, after remaining still for a few more minutes, had attempted to move his hands. Every coma patient comes out of it differently. Some experience extensive brain damage, while others appear completely normal, having the impression they had just taken a long nap. There was no definitive way to be certain, but pulling against the restraints was a very good sign.

The doctor had been on call for most of the night and was exhausted. He was well aware of the current state of the healthcare system, and like any other business, it was driven by a balance sheet. He spent most shifts doing his best to tend to his patients, but his efforts were mostly patchwork. Fix them up quickly and discharge them. Keeping beds available was of paramount importance. Sure, he had saved many lives, which was what had inspired him to become a physician in the first place, but it didn't take long for him to realize that his occupation felt more like working on an assembly line than pursuing any higher calling.

He had spent countless nights trying to convince himself, usually after the third scotch and while alone in his kitchen, that he was making a difference, but that had become a much more difficult sell. The doctor had long since ceased following up on his patients' outcomes. Occasionally, he would inquire about the status of a particularly bad one.

Six months ago, while wrapping up his shift and completing paperwork for the bean counters, a forty-year-old male involved in a single-vehicle crash was wheeled in by the paramedics. The man had collided with the cement median barrier on the 401 highway just outside of Pickering, resulting in a spectacular nine full rotations before coming to a stop by the roadside. No other vehicles were involved (which was a blessing as they didn't have the beds). The doctor worked on him for twenty minutes before handing him over to the surgical trauma team.

The man survived. It turned out he was a personal injury lawyer. In this case, the doctor's follow-up wasn't purely altruistic; he also aimed to assess the potential for a pending malpractice lawsuit. Although rare in Canada, they still happened. In the end, there were none. It turned out that this near-death experience had a deep impact on the man, leading him to abandon his ambulance-chasing ways and dedicate his life to Jesus Christ. The doctor had seen this type of thing before. Typically lasting a month or two, then patients would go right back to where they were once the stint in rehab was over. The simple truth was that Jesus didn't pay as well as a lawyer's hourly rate.

This one, however, piqued his interest. Like most physicians, he was a sucker for a genuine mystery, and now that the patient was awake, he hoped to get some answers.

The doctor stood at the foot of the bed, observing the night nurse as she held a cup of water to the patient's cracked lips. Only a small amount of water at a time. Too much at this stage could lead to complications.

"Welcome back, Mr. Meeks," the doctor said, glancing over

Leigh's chart.

"What happened to me?" Leigh croaked, a beat between words.

"Well, that's the million-dollar question, isn't it? We were hoping you might be able to shed some light on that yourself. But we can discuss all that later. Rest first, talk later, yes?"

Leigh nodded, taking another painful sip of water.

"The good news is you don't appear to have sustained any lasting damage from the coma."

Coma.

"We will need to run a whole lot of additional tests, but you appear to be in good shape," the doctor reassured him. Leigh was now summitting the Glasgow Coma Scale. Leigh tugged against the restraints.

"Oh, yes. It's just a precaution, Mr. Meeks. I suppose you won't get very far if we remove them. Nurse." He nodded, granting permission.

"I'm sure you have many questions, Mr. Meeks, as do I, but all in due time," the doctor said, returning Leigh's chart to the footboard of the bed. "I will check in on you later to see how you're doing. If you need anything, press the call button, and a nurse will—" In a whisper, Leigh interrupted, "Is there anyone waiting to see me?"

"Oh, yes. I almost forgot. There is someone very anxious to speak with you. I assured them that as soon as you woke up, I would notify them, and I have. They won't be long," the doctor said. Leigh groaned, barely audible to anyone in the room. He supposed he was as ready for them as he would ever be.

"Yes, well. I have instructed them to keep the visit brief. As you are under my care, I will be the one setting the rules regarding visitation. That said, I suppose a minute or two won't do any harm," the doctor said.

Leigh attempted a nod, his neck aching. The doctor's pager buzzed. He removed the small, black box from his belt and checked the number.

"So long, Mr. Meeks. We'll talk again soon. And remember,

for now, just bed rest," he nodded at the nurse and left the room.

The nurse adjusted the tubes protruding from his arm, checked something under the bed, and entered a code into the vital signs monitor. As she opened the door to leave, she took a step back, slightly startled. Closing the door behind her, Leigh could hear a muffled, one-sided conversation.

"Hello. Yes, he's awake. Only a few minutes now. Doctor's orders," she said.

"He's awake? Oh, thank God." It was Charlotte.

CHAPTER 39

My doctors have suggested keeping a journal, but I expressed a preference for letters, so I decided to write to you. They believe writing things down might aid in improving my memory.

I have remained coma-free, they call it, for nine days now. After emerging from the first coma, I experienced a relapse that lasted another full twelve hours, although I have no memory of the interval between the two comas.

Apart from the memory loss, I appear to be in good physical condition and my physicians are still at a loss to explain the initial cause of the coma. While my short-term memory seems to be functioning well, I have a great deal of difficulty recalling the events that led up to the coma.

I'm happy to be home, but I'm bored bored bored. Aside from Charlotte, no friends have visited or called, which strikes me as peculiar. I can't even recall if I have friends at all. Nonetheless, it was nice to see Charlotte. She travelled from New York and has chosen to stay in town until she has me settled in. She's staying down the road at the Park Plaza Hotel. We have yet to discuss my next novel, though I know it's on her mind.

Charlotte has been able to fill me in on a few things. It appears that before the coma, I would sometimes fall silent during our phone calls, which she now believes was me nodding off. Sometimes even mid-sentence, if you can imagine that. She had come straight from the airport to the hospital to see me, but it seems I experienced a relapse while she waited in the hall.

The doctors are currently investigating this nodding-off thing as a potential connection. These episodes continue post-coma, and because of this, I have been banned from driving.

A peculiar development has occurred: I find myself smoking more than ever, and consuming alcohol makes me feel ill. After returning home from the hospital, I had a glass of red wine and, approximately fifteen minutes later, I vomited in the toilet. The smoking, however, does not seem to affect me at all.

However, the reason I'm writing to you is not related to these matters. I need to get something off my chest, and although I trust Charlotte, I cannot risk the possibility of what I'm about to disclose ending up in the newspapers or with the powers that be at the publisher. Nevertheless, I feel the need to share it.

I think I might be going insane.

Ever since the coma, I have been experiencing these terrible nightmares. These nightmares are chronic and recurrent, and occur each and every time I fall asleep. Always the same, with the slightest alterations here and there and they happen every time I fall asleep. They are so vivid. The most intense ones happen when I manage to get a solid eight or nine hours of sleep. They seem to go on forever, and when I wake up, it takes me some time to reorient myself.

Whenever I have what Charlotte calls a nod, the nightmare resurfaces, lasting only a few minutes.

In these dreams, it's always nighttime, and I am being pursued. I am uncertain by whom or what. I am constantly in extreme danger, and always on the run. Usually, I find myself in abandoned buildings, like warehouses, but sometimes this changes too. I have also dreamt of subway trains, twenty-four-hour doughnut shops, and parks. In every dream, people are always moving away from me.

In the dream, I am sick. I have caught glimpses of my reflection and discovered I am emaciated and filthy. I look homeless and desperately in need of hospitalization. I am always drinking alcohol. It seems I always have a never-ending bottle of vodka within reach, refilling itself in each subsequent dream. Sometimes I find myself screaming about God knows what or smashing windows in abandoned buildings. I am also addicted to drugs, evident from a bag of pills stuck in my sock. And without fail, the last action I take in every dream, regardless of my location or activities, is to take a couple of these pills before I wake up. The dream always ends the same way: reaching for the baggie, taking a few pills, and washing them down with alcohol.

I am also afraid that I might commit suicide in the dream. It feels like I might. I am now terrified of falling asleep. I experience the visceral sensations of homelessness, hunger, and constant fear for my life. I wish it would stop. In an attempt to sleep as little as possible, I have ramped up my coffee intake since the dreams began.

Charlotte has told me that she needs to travel this weekend due to a personal matter. Although I offered to accompany her, just for a change of scenery, she refused, believing I should stay home and rest. She's probably right.

Most of my memory lapses I have kept to myself. While I have had to disclose some of them to the docs, the dreams remain a secret.

Charlotte is dealing with a family issue. I have managed to gather information in dribs and drabs, but for the most part, I am simply going with the flow. I believe she is worried about a troubled family member, though she may have already mentioned it, and I can't remember. Maybe I should ask, but I don't. She departs on Friday, leaving me alone with no one to distract me this weekend. Just me and my dreams. Lucky me.

Love,
Ranleigh

CHAPTER 40

The sky changed colour from tangerine to a blanket of dark purple as the plane touched down. Against his doctors' advice, Leigh decided to take the wheel and drive himself to the hotel. It was too late to show up unannounced on some stranger's doorstep, so he had gone ahead and booked a room. He figured he would track down Charlotte first thing in the morning once he had a night's sleep.

The man Leigh had travelled all this way for lived way off the beaten track. Earlier in the week, Charlotte finally revealed where she was headed and why. Turns out, a family member had been holed up in a rehab center, dealing with addiction. According to Charlotte, he was doing better now and had been released a few weeks ago. But of course, his place had to be halfway across the country, so Leigh braced himself for the two-hour drive from the airport. His main concern? Staying awake. To combat that, he guzzled cup after cup of black coffee on the flight, hoping he would hold.

After what felt like an eternity of driving, the new Guide Star navigation system bolted to the dashboard of the rental car blurted out instructions like a droning vice principal on the school PA, letting him know he'd reach the hotel in roughly twenty minutes.

Staring into the dark abyss ahead, Leigh could make out the faint flickering lights of a small town. It was too dark to see any details of the buildings, except for one. A run-down wooden structure with a coned roof loomed over the town like a giant. The building dwarfed the town, standing sentry beside the railway tracks. If only Leigh hadn't been so fixated on that building, and if only the moon had shed a bit more light, he might have noticed the road sign he blew past on his right.

**THANK YOU FOR VISITING
THE TOWN OF KINGLIN
Pop. 835
Come and see us again, real soon!**

CHAPTER 41

I made it here all right. This isn't the best hotel I've ever stayed in, but it's adequate. I'm only planning to stay for two nights, so I can manage. Since there's no room service, I've ordered local delivery. I had hoped I could report that the dreams have stopped, but sadly, that's not the case. If anything, they're getting worse.

During the plane ride here, I felt a sudden urge to share what's been happening with Charlotte once I catch up to her. Luckily, I had time on the car ride from the airport to reflect on it and have decided against it. I have this sneaking suspicion that if I revealed what's going on inside my head, Charlotte might feel compelled to make an unannounced visit to my doctor. They would probably have me committed to the bug factory, where I would spend the rest of my days working on my basket weaving skills. On the other hand, my book sales might go through the roof.

They can't last forever, can they, these dreams? So for now, I'll just have to suffer through. The terrifying thought I can't shake is that if I die in one of these dreams, I might fall back into another coma, and permanently. Die in a dream and go into a coma? Maybe I should walk under a few ladders while I'm at it. Just some unpleasant nightmares and that's all they are.

The locations have changed a bit. It seems I've moved on from the abandoned building to an empty storage locker. There's nothing in there except for a ratty old sleeping bag and what appears to be a battery-powered camping lantern, like one of those Canadian Tire jobs. The night before last, I seemed to be back on the subway, but last night was a particularly bad one. They do seem to be getting worse. Did I mention that? I sat cross-legged on the sleeping bag in the storage locker, the lantern mostly illuminating everything below my elbows. The corners and ceiling of the square box were completely blacked out. It felt like I was floating in space. The gym bag I've been carrying around made another appearance, crumpled beside me like a sleeping, pet dog.

In the dream, I was in a particularly bad way, taking long gulps of vodka and talking to myself. Well, crying to myself, is probably more accurate. It went on like this for hours until, at one point, I reached into the bag and found a gun. I sat there, looking at it for a long time, cradling it in my filthy, shaking hands, until finally, I pointed it at my face and jammed the barrel into my mouth. Tears streamed down my cheeks and the metal ground down on my fillings. I couldn't stop gagging. I remember feeling a strong panic, and no matter how hard I tried, I couldn't do anything about it. I just had to ride it out. So, if this joker actually sees fit to pull the trigger, then I guess I'm off on another trip to Coma Country.

*But it never happened. I just put the gun back in the bag and cried again. And the most peculiar part of the nightmare is this: Just before I woke up, and I mean just before, **I looked at my watch** and fished more pills from the small bag. I washed them down with more vodka, and then I woke up. As I think I mentioned before, every dream ends with the pills. But this is the first time I remember looking at my watch. Curious.*

Anyway, probably goes without saying that I'm really looking forward to a good, long sleep tonight. Haha. I plan to set out tomorrow after breakfast, and I hope everything goes well for her...

Sibling.

Yes, that's it. A brother. I'm not sure where that memory came from or why, but she's here to check on a brother who just got out of rehab. It seems the doctors were right after all. Maybe the letter writing works. Maybe my memory is returning.

There's the pizza.

Love,
Ranleigh

CHAPTER 42

The Boarding house sat on the outskirts of Fairlawn City.

After a full night's sleep, a half-out-of-his-wits Ranleigh Meeks felt immense gratitude for being awake and didn't care where. Just being upright, with wide-open eyes, was all he needed, thank you very much. To ensure he would remain this way, he consumed four cups of black coffee for breakfast, taking out extra insurance. From his room, he called his publisher to find out Charlotte's whereabouts. Charlotte, a dedicated agent, would never dream of being unreachable for an hour, let alone a full day. Pulling the rental car out of the empty parking lot, Leigh struggled to push last night's nightmare out of his mind.

Leigh preferred a silent drive. The radio held no interest for him. He was mulling over a few things Charlotte had told him about her brother that came back while downing his third cup of coffee over breakfast. He remembered her mentioning earlier in the week that her brother had done well in rehab, passing with flying colours. He had been like a new man. During their phone conversations, she recalled how it was between them when they were children. Before this latest attempt at sobriety, when his drinking and drug use had spiraled out of control, and just before she cut him off for *the last time*, they never really talked. She felt he would merely be waiting for her to stop talking so he could reclaim the spotlight. In the later stages of this last go around, all he wanted was money. However, treatment had brought about a change. On one of their last phone calls, he had actually listened to *her*. She told him about her job, the latest novel she was working on with Ranleigh, and her life. But this brief halcyon respite was not to last. Around the time doctors at the hospital were waiting for Ranleigh to wake up, Charlotte's brother stopped answering his phone. At first, Charlotte told herself he was busy with his recovery. But as the week progressed, she started to worry. He remembered that as soon as her calls to her brother transitioned from the answering machine to a disconnected line, she booked a flight.

Fighting the urge to nod, Ranleigh pulled up to the Boarding house. Ranleigh found lately that most people engaged in conversations like they were desperately in need of a washroom - urgent, mostly one-sided exchanges of information. However, the Boarding house manager was refreshingly different.

Cardboard.

The word flashed in his mind, momentarily distracting him from the manager's last sentence.

"Can I help you?" the man asked.

"Sorry, yes. Hello. My name is Ranleigh Meeks, and I'm here looking for a friend of mine," Ranleigh replied.

"You're the writer? Well, I'll be. I'll say, it's an honour to have you here. And I'm guessing you're not looking to rent a room," the man said, shifting his oversized frame in his seat.

"Can't say that I am," Ranleigh said.

Ranleigh instantly liked the man, who exuded a self-assured yet calm and friendly manner. He seemed like someone you could confide in, someone who would never judge. The man introduced himself as Lardon. "Well, what can I do for you?" Lardon asked.

"I've come all this way because, frankly, I'm concerned about a colleague of mine who might have come by here yesterday, looking for her brother," Ranleigh said.

"Sure. She was here. Pretty lady. Polite. I have to tell you, though, she left disappointed. As for the brother, we haven't seen him around for the better part of two weeks. And he's late on rent. Again." Ranleigh nodded. "He was gone for a few months a while back, and he asked me to hold his spot. The rent checks kept coming by mail, signed by the sister. She works with you, you say?"

"She does," Leigh replied.

"Well, I might be talking outta school here, but I suppose it don't matter much one way or the next." Mr. Lardon examined Ranleigh, assessing his commitment to keeping a confidence, then continued, "The brother, he came back from wherever he was all that time. He looked good and acted like a born-again Christian. Spent a lot of time in the taverns around here, looking for fresh recruits. Can't say there's a shortage here, mind you. Don't get me wrong—I'm as behind a man as anyone can be when a person wants to get up on the wagon and stay there for good. But that boy was on FIRE," Lardon said.

"From drunk to monk," Leigh mumbled to himself. Lardon served up a hearty laugh.

"Got to remember that one," he said, slapping the desk. "Yep, just like that."

"Well, thanks for your time, Mr. Lardon," Leigh said, rising to his feet. "One quick question before I go?"

"Shoot," Lardon said.

"Any chance I can get a look at his room?"

"That's not something I'm supposed to do. It's still private property, even if he's behind on rent."

"I'll tell you what, Mr. Lardon. I'll pay off what's owed on the rent and throw in an extra fifty. How about then?" Ranleigh retrieved his wallet from his back pocket.

Lardon unlocked the door of a large cupboard behind him, revealing rows of single keys with circular number tags. The numbers were handwritten. He removed key number 5, closed the door, and squeezed the padlock shut. Turning back to Ranleigh, he took a good, long look before speaking.

"Jimmy's looking for you, Leigh," he said.

"You mean Charlotte. Yes, she probably is." Leigh chalked the slip to a senior moment.

The first thing that hit them was the stench – the smell of rotten meat and sour milk. For a second, Ranleigh wondered if it could be the smell of the brother's decaying body, but that seemed unlikely. Covering their mouths, Ranleigh and Lardon entered the room, careful to keep the door open. Ranleigh leaned against the counter beside the sink for support as he surveyed the room. It served as a living room, dining room, and kitchen, all rolled into one. The small sink overflowed with cheap, dirty plates and glasses. However, it was the items on the table that told the story. Dirty promotional glasses from fast-food joints were haphazardly pushed against the window. The linoleum floor was covered in broken glass and long brown smears. *Is that shit?* Ranleigh wondered.

"Looks like blood," Lardon said, reading his mind.

The table was cluttered with drug paraphernalia - tinfoil, long glass pipes with blackened, bulbous ends reminiscent of the mercury-drinking bird Leigh had as a child. The mercury would cause the bird to dip forward towards a glass of water, giving the impression of drinking. Also on the table was a pile of empty Ziplock baggies and several aluminum cans. On the bench beneath the tables, a surplus of porn magazines was strewn about, some open, others scattered on the floor.

"I've seen enough," Ranleigh said, turning towards the exit.

As Ranleigh was leaving, his attention was drawn to the only object in the room that came close to normal. Hung on the wall beside the window was a framed photograph. The picture, although old and faded, displayed a clear image. It featured a teenage boy and a young girl posing in front of a pickup truck. The boy had rolled up the sleeve of his t-shirt, flexing a pale white bicep next to the tan of his forearm. The girl rested her chin on his shoulder, sticking her tongue out at the camera. It was a snapshot of much happier times. He assumed the girl in the picture was Charlotte, but it was the boy who captured his attention.

Captivated, he took a few steps toward the photograph, being careful not to slip on the garbage, broken glass, or blood or shit or whatever it was. Leaning in, Ranleigh examined the faces closely. He knew the boy but couldn't place him. The face filled him with a sense of dread, like cold fingers stroking the back of his neck. It was no use. The gaps in his memory still prevented him from remembering.

Emerging into the sunlight and the much-needed fresh air, Leigh joined Lardon.

"God bless Brad McGinnis," Lardon said to no one in particular.

Brad.

It came back then. Standing in front of that dilapidated, shithole of a building, he remembered —the fire, the rodeo, the teenagers, and their leader. A boy named Brad.

PART SIX

BLACKOUT

CHAPTER 43

Two days had passed since he had put the gun in his mouth, hoping to find the courage to end it. But Leigh couldn't bring himself to do it. Now he spent most of his time sleeping, though he couldn't be certain of the exact number of hours, maybe eighteen? He rarely left the empty storage locker where a sympathetic security guard with a grizzled face and an advanced case of age-related hyperkyphosis allowed him to stay temporarily. But he knew he would have to leave when the unit was rented out.

In the dream place, Leigh no longer had control over his actions. Someone else was in charge. The dark locker room had become like his own private movie theatre, where he helplessly watched the film play out on the surrounding walls. Day after day, he witnessed scenes of his recovery in a hospital, boarding a plane, and renting a car at an airport kiosk. But the film would sometimes abruptly stop, plunging Leigh into darkness. He would crouch in the corner of the locker, shivering and waiting for the next reel, a hotel room, pizza, and a warm shower.

After another night of cowering, drinking, and playing with the gun, Leigh prepared himself for another double feature. He took out the baggy from his sock and swallowed a small handful of pills, he no longer counted how many he took. Leigh swallowed the capsules and nestled deep inside the warm sleeping bag. He extinguished the lantern, ready to float away. And float away he did. Unfortunately for Leigh, the management was busy hanging a sign on the movie marquee: THEATRE CLOSED UNTIL FURTHER NOTICE.

Though Leigh's dependency on alcohol and OxyContin was now completely beyond his control, curiously he had yet to experience a *blackout*. During a blackout, users lose all conscious awareness of their actions while intoxicated and when they come out of it, they come out with no memory of where they've been or what they've done. It is a terrifying ordeal for the user, as they engage in activities, make decisions, and act without any recollection whatsoever. Addicts have been known to drive cars, contact ex-lovers, or even attack strangers, with no memory of the events. Often, they come to at the most inconvenient moments, sometimes finding themselves in extremely hazardous situations. It feels akin to waking up safe and sound in your bed, only to discover you're behind the wheel of a car, roaring down the highway at twice the speed limit, in the wrong direction in the middle of the night.

People experiencing blackouts have called their bosses in the middle of the night, unloading strings of abuses. Ex-lovers have rekindled long-dead romances, regardless of their current marital status. The one commonality among blackouts is that users engage in stupid, dangerous, and often tragic actions and frequently all three.

Leigh had expected to enter the dream place as usual, even if only to watch the movie. After taking the pills, Leigh neither stayed awake nor entered the dream place. Instead, he fell deep into a genuine blackout, creating a chasm between the nightmarish reality he lived in and the dream life he experienced. Instantly, both sides began operating simultaneously but independently, causing everything to just fall apart.

Just as Dream Ranleigh was ordering breakfast at the hotel,

Reality Leigh was busy packing the gym bag he had stolen from Jimmy. Of course, he had no awareness that he was doing so, but he seemed to zip the bag with a sense of purpose, appearing to have a plan.

Momentarily blinded by the daylight, Leigh's vision adjusted as he scanned the empty factory street up and down. Performing a completely unconscious, yet quick calculation, he estimated he was in for an hour's walk. He hadn't had a decent meal in days, yet despite being shaky from hunger and dehydration, he walked remarkably fast, resembling a determined sleepwalker, whistling to the rhythm of his footsteps, all while in the midst of a severe blackout.

And while Dream Ranleigh was investigating Brad McGinnis's disappearance with Mr. Lardon, Reality Leigh was weaving his way through the streets of Toronto. Instead of consuming something sensible, Leigh drank the last of his vodka and consumed the remaining pills. Leigh was on the verge of an overdose, and if it hadn't been for this miraculous autopilot propelling him forward, he might have expired right there on the spot.

Ranleigh carefully bagged most of the garbage, careful not to stick himself with any stray needles, and stuffed the bags into the rental car's trunk. Considering the circumstances, Lardon had been more than reasonable and agreed not to involve the police regarding the drugs found in the room, as long as the outstanding rent was paid in full. Ranleigh cleaned up for Charlotte's sake. He figured Charlotte had dealt with enough of Brad's messes. Mercifully, Lardon had kept her out of the room.

He was almost there. He could sense it. No, he could *smell* it. Leigh pulled hard on an invisible leash that tried to hold him back, the drugs were slowing him down, but he was determined to finish it.

About a block south of the gym on Yonge Street, he spotted Stas struggling to extricate his oversized body from a low-sitting sports car. Stas hadn't noticed the homeless man approaching him. If he had recognized Leigh, he would have been surprised to see the man he had been searching for all this time, coming right toward him— the man who had shot his bodyguard, stolen from him, humiliated him in front of the strippers and flattened his nose into permanent disfigurement. If Stas had known, he would have killed Leigh right there on the street, giving the patrons of the House of Lords hair design quite a show.

But it was Leigh who reached into a bag, feeling for the gun, a white froth forming at the corners of his mouth. Rounding a parked car, Leigh felt a presence behind his left shoulder. Two hands grabbed him by the scruff of his jacket, nearly lifting him off his feet. Leigh was dragged into the doorway of a defunct head shop. The disembodied hands swung him around, causing Leigh to instinctively raise his arms defensively, leaning against a window that had been whitewashed with the words "FOR LEASE." Although still unconscious and operating in a complete blackout, Leigh seemed to recognize the man.

"You need to follow me," the man said.

"The fuck I do," Leigh slurred, trying to straighten himself. "Get out of my way! I'm going to kill that son of a bitch and put an end to all of this," Leigh said.

"You need to follow me," the man repeated.

After completing the cleanup, Lardon saw Ranleigh off to the rental car. He told him how sorry he was for Ranleigh's troubles, collected the rent money, and wished him well. As Ranleigh rolled down the driveway, he noticed Mr. Lardon in the rearview mirror, waving him back. Slowing the car to a stop, Ranleigh lowered the window as Mr. Lardon caught up to the driver's side.

"I wasn't gonna say anything, but I have a brother of my

own back home, and I can only imagine what she must be going through. So here it is. Might be a long shot, but it's a starting place. There's a pocket-sized town about ten minutes down the highway. You probably drove right past it when you came in from the airport. Blink and you miss it. Apparently, back in the day, it used to be a nice place to settle down, but that was a long time ago. Now it's a shithole. Some diehards have stayed there out of bullheaded determination, and others have stayed put because they have no other options. Anyway, you hear it all in a boarding house, and I've heard that and then some. In the town I'm talking about, there's a big house. Been abandoned for years. Kids go there to party and fool around. I guess they figure nobody's going to disturb them in a place like that, and they're probably right. It might not be much to go on, but it didn't seem to me like Mr. McGinnis could have made it very far in his condition, so it might be worth a look. You'll find it on Kramden if memory serves. You can't miss it," Lardon said.

"Thanks, Mr. Lardon," Ranleigh said, sliding the car into drive.

Rolling away from the boarding house, Ranleigh wondered why he didn't head directly to the address Lardon had given him.

Because you need rest, he thought. *You've had enough bad news for one morning. If he's there, then he won't be going anywhere soon. Just head back to the hotel, grab something to eat, and take a quick nap. Think this through. You need some time. And you need some sleep.*

Sleep. Ranleigh shuddered.

While Reality Leigh debated the finer points of not killing a man in broad daylight in the middle of Yonge Street, Dream Ranleigh took off his shoes and curled up on the hotel bed.

CHAPTER 44

Afraid of falling asleep but too exhausted to resist, Ranleigh
drifted off on the hotel room bed. The dream consisted mostly
of blank space. Occasionally stirring to change his position,
Ranleigh would awaken to the hum of the air conditioner,
feeling immense relief as he realized, for once, he hadn't been
dreaming. It wasn't until later, in that just-before-waking-for-
good place, that the nightmare caught up to him in bright
technicolour.

He sensed his body dying. A frothy foam dribbled down his
chin, understanding that he might not survive the next few
minutes. Helpless to take any action, he likened the experience
to two cars speeding towards the apex of a corner from
opposite directions, oblivious to the imminent crash.

Later, he would recall trying desperately to wake himself up.
Then, there was Mr. Lardon crossing the street, heading
directly towards him. Although he didn't resemble himself
much, it was him. He was taller, younger, and more muscular
than when they had met earlier that day, wearing a pair of dirty
denim overalls. Seizing Ranleigh by the scruff of his jacket,
Lardon told him to come along, dragging him out of the street.
Despite Lardon's frantic efforts to drag Ranleigh to safety, he
refused to go.

Why wouldn't I go? Do I want to die?

In horror, Ranleigh watched helplessly as he rejected the only lifeline available to him. Desperate, he attempted to alter the dream from the inside, a task much more difficult than it seems. At first, nothing happened. The homeless Ranleigh in the dream continued to burn his only bridge to safety. But, gradually, with his mind strained to the breaking point, Ranleigh seemed to gain control over himself within the dream. He managed to propel his dream self forward, in a direction he chose - straight towards Lardon.

As if sleepwalking, Ranleigh followed Lardon into a doughnut shop.

CHAPTER 45

Ranleigh stirred, alone in the hotel room in Fairlawn City. He reached for his cigarettes, attempting to process what had happened to him the past twenty-four hours. He wasn't doing well. How could the man he now sought be the same kid from that summer at his grandmother's? And if Charlotte was his sister, wouldn't that mean they had crossed paths as children that summer? Maybe that day at the rodeo? Could this be the Brad responsible for the deaths of Verna Hewitt and Dallas Cooper?

While changing his clothes, he vowed not to share any of these epiphanies with Charlotte until he had time to sort through them. And where was Charlotte anyway? Surely, he would have caught up with her by now. He knew she had been to the boarding house and spoken to Mr. Lardon, but then what? Over his third cup of coffee, he made a second promise to himself. He would not sleep until he felt sure that he could save himself from his dreams.

Driving into Kinglin from Fairlawn City, Ranleigh found himself captivated by what he saw. The buildings, once hazy in his memory or not there at all, now brought back memories of the week he had spent with his grandmother in 1979.

The landscape had changed very little. The grain elevator,

the pavilion, and the Drive-In still stood, while GREEN'S Grocery store and the bank had long been shuttered. As he turned off the main street and headed for the Hewitt house on Kramden, his stomach fluttered. When had his grandmother passed away? He couldn't remember. He had no memory of attending a funeral here. Did he even know about it? Was he given the chance to grieve her? The place in his mind that should access these memories remained strictly off-limits to Ranleigh, and the more he tried to remember, the further they slipped away.

The GPS device guided him directly to Kramden. *If they had these devices back then, the firemen might have found the house and probably saved Verna Hewitt*, he thought. And if not Verna, Dallas Cooper would surely have survived.

Slowing the car to a crawl, Ranleigh took in the street before him. He knew this had been the better part of town when the Bee Gees topped the charts and Burt Reynolds was the biggest movie star in the world.

The houses stood larger and with superior construction than the others in town, but decay had silently crept in when nobody was looking. Neglect lingered here. Ranleigh couldn't make out if any of the houses were inhabited. The grass had grown too high on most of the lawns, and half of the windows were boarded up. Approaching his destination, Ranleigh Meeks noticed a small figure sitting on the curb behind another rental car, legs splayed, elbows on knees, head in hands.

It was Charlotte.

CHAPTER 46

Coming out of the blackout, Leigh's eyes opened, expecting to see the squalor of the storage container, but instead, he was confronted by the image of a familiar face, Ron. Panic surged within him as Leigh desperately needed to get away from him. He attempted to rise, but his legs failed. Ron reached out and grabbed his forearm to keep him from falling off the chair.

"Take a seat, Leigh," Ron said. Left with little choice, Leigh reluctantly sat back down, struggling to free his arm from Ron's vice-like grip. As the room came into focus, Leigh found himself facing Ron at a small round table in a doughnut shop. To Leigh's left, was an empty counter with four mushroom stools. Behind the counter racks of doughnuts. The sprinkled ones caught his attention. Leigh thought about his pills.

"What happened?" Leigh asked, keeping his gaze fixed on the coffee cup in front of him.

"I found you out on Yonge, heading towards the gym. After you left the meeting, I called Jimmy, who gave me the name of your dealer. He didn't give that up easy. I've been looking for you ever since. I had the day off and thought I'd give the gym another shot. See if you had been around trying to pick up. Guess we just got lucky." Leigh listened, his eyes never leaving the coffee cup, while Ron continued.

"I don't know what to tell you, Leigh. I don't know how bad this has to get. But I do know this— only you are going to know when you've had enough. For some people, losing a job or a spouse is enough, while others need to land themselves in jail or the hospital before they truly see things for what they are. With you, it seems like you need to dig a deeper hole than most. You're a tough nut, Leigh," Ron said.

Leigh leaned his face down towards the coffee cup and took a sip of the steaming liquid.

"If losing your job, living on the streets and being this sick isn't enough, and you're still not there, then for God's sake have something to eat before you go," Ron said, sliding a steaming bowl of soup across the table.

"I can't," Leigh finally confessed.

"Can't or won't?" Ron asked.

"What's the fucking difference? I'm so tired," Leigh said.

"Tired is good. We can work with tired."

"I only went with you that night to get back my pills," Leigh confessed, his hand trembling as he gripped a spoon.

"I know," Ron said.

"You tricked me. I hated that place you took me. I hated their shit-eating grins. I hated them, and I hated you for taking me there."

"No tricks, Leigh," Ron said.

"Sure," Leigh replied.

"You are dying. Do you know that?"

"I know."

"Do you even want to live?" Ron asked.

"Not like this," Leigh said, dropping the spoon onto the table.

"And the pills? You think they help with that?"

"Not anymore. Not anymore," Leigh replied. With that realization came the tears. Leigh felt like he would never stop crying.

CHAPTER 47

The girl lifted her head from her hands and waved at the rental car. Ranleigh pressed his foot down on the brake and put the car in park. The girl stood, brushed off the seat of her pants, and turned towards Ranleigh. She appeared to be about ten years old, with shiny chestnut-coloured hair razor-parted in the middle and tucked behind her ears.

As she approached the car, Ranleigh could see the faded Charlie's Angels iron-on transfer, with the border sparkles dulled and peeling at the edges. Ranleigh rolled down his window. They locked eyes for a long time. Ranleigh couldn't comprehend what he was seeing. His head hurt, and he felt drowsy. He prayed another nod wouldn't come on.

"Depressing, huh?" the kid said. "Must be a little further on up the road."

"Yeah, I think it's just up there. I've been there before."

"I'm game. But listen, Ranleigh. Maybe we should just forget the whole thing and turn around. Whatdya think?" Charlotte placed her hands on the car door.

"Why would you say that? We've come all this way," Ranleigh replied.

"I dunno," the kid said, cracking her gum. "Call it a feeling."

"Yeah," Ranleigh began to nod off.

"You don't look so hot," Charlotte said. "Want me to get you some help?"

"I'll be okay. I think I just need to sleep for a bit," Ranleigh replied.

"When my brother got back into rehab this time, I thought it would work. I dunno. I guess I was wrong." The words sounded strange coming from a kid's mouth. "I should have known better, but I wanted to *believe him*. I wanted to believe that all the things he was telling me were true. I wanted to believe that things would be different. Better." Ranleigh was fading fast.

"We all want to believe, Charlotte," Ranleigh managed.

"Yeah, I guess we do," she said as she propped her elbows on the car door between the two pillars, cradling her jaw in her hands.

To stay awake, Ranleigh tried to focus on her chipped nail polish. "I've never doubted that recovery works. I doubt Brad. I doubt him, but I don't want to give up on him, you know?" She cracked the gum again. "I dunno, maybe I just feel guilty about how things went down."

Sliding down in his seat, Ranleigh struggled to stay awake.

"We only lived together until I was about nine years old. My parent's marriage had run its course by then. My mother never wanted to live in a small town like this; she was far too ambitious, and my dad liked to drink. Maybe that's where Brad got it from, who knows? When they split, they divided us too. Girls with girls and boys with boys, or at least that was the wisdom in 1978, and this happened to a lot of families. My mom and I moved to Winnipeg, and Brad stayed here. After we left him, my dad's drinking got worse. He died of cirrhosis in the eighties. I grew up and moved to New York. Brad stayed and made out as best he could. So, I feel guilty and so I pay for the rehab."

In his haze, Ranleigh wondered how a nine-year-old kid pays for anyone's rehab.

"And maybe he's dead in there. And if so, then maybe it's

my fault, and I don't think that I can handle that," she said.

As Dream Ranleigh fell asleep in the car, Reality Leigh had come out of his blackout in a doughnut shop.

CHAPTER 48

Getting to Ron's apartment took half an hour by subway. The two men had spent an hour talking in the doughnut shop before Ron suggested that Leigh come to his place. With nowhere else to go and the rage towards Stas subsiding, Leigh agreed. Where the fuck else was he going to go? Ron promised him that he wouldn't hammer him with any more recovery speak and that Leigh could stay with him as long as he needed to get his shit together, on the condition that drugs or alcohol were off the menu at Ron's place.

The apartment, small and practically empty, was furnished with items that appeared to have come from the Goodwill. The worn sofa did its best to prop up sagging cushions, and Leigh could feel the springs when he sat down. He found himself missing his apartment in the Colonnade. Against the only window, a small bookshelf displayed the obligatory recovery books, including a well-worn hardcover edition of Alcoholics Anonymous. Ron's sobriety medallions were proudly displayed on top of the shelf, alongside a potted plant. There was no television. The plant was alive.

Ron asked if Leigh wanted something to eat or another coffee, but Leigh declined. They sat in silence, both feeling no need to engage in small talk, which would have been absurd given the circumstances. Leigh was certain that Ron could have gone on for hours about the benefits of a sober life if given the chance, but Leigh was too exhausted to absorb any more platitudes, slogans, or steps.

To break the uncomfortable silence, Ron went to the kitchenette and prepared a cheese sandwich for Leigh. Because of his size, Ron looked like a child playing with a toy kitchen. Leigh wasn't hungry but was grateful for the effort.

Ron asked Leigh if he would like to take a shower. Ron's clothes wouldn't fit him of course, but he kept an extra set of regular-sized clothes for the men he sponsored, broken men who needed a place to stay, a meal, or a shower. These acts of kindness touched Leigh. While on the couch, he tried to figure out Ron's angle, but perhaps there simply weren't any.

"Speaking of sponsees," Ron said, "I need to step out for a few hours if you think you won't die on me while I'm out." Leigh waved a hand, indicating that he'd be fine if Ron had to leave.

"I have a newcomer I'm working with. He's a lot like you. He came to us through a court order mandating attendance at meetings. He was arrested for a third DUI. Crack is his thing. Very tricky to get off of, that shit. The court-ordered newbies are the worst. This usually only works if they come on their own steam. They might be able to stay off long enough to satisfy the courts and pass the urine tests, but once they're out of the jackpot they put themselves in, they usually go right back. But you can never give up on them. There's a guy in my group who picked up his first desire chip in 1969, and just last year, we celebrated his very first one-year medallion. Took him twenty-eight years to put together one year of continuous sobriety, and he's looking good. So, I never give up on anyone, and they would never give up on me."

Leigh nodded as Ron spoke. Not much of this was making it into his damaged mind, but at least he wasn't on about God or those infantile slogans. This time, Ron's words seemed more real.

"Anyway, I promised I wouldn't get on you with program

speak, so that's enough from me," Ron said as he threw on a ratty jacket and headed for the door. "The shower is over there. It's not hard to find. You'll see a set of clothes, a clean towel, and a new toothbrush on a shelf beside the sink. I shouldn't be gone more than a few hours. Mostly, this guy just listens politely until I sign his piece of paper, but you never know."

Before Ron left the apartment, Leigh spoke up, "And you're okay me being here? You're not worried I might rob you blind?"

"What's there to steal?" Ron replied with a smile. "Listen, Leigh, you could certainly take my stuff and head back out there to try to pick up and that's your choice, but I hope you stay. Maybe sleep on it for a bit? The drugs will still be out there when you wake up. Always are. I'll see you later."

With that, he opened the door and left Leigh alone.

After taking a long, hot shower and eating half a cheese sandwich, Leigh fell asleep on Ron's couch.

CHAPTER 49

After losing consciousness in his car with Charlotte waiting at the window, Ranleigh tumbled instantly down the rabbit hole.

He dreamed of Lardon who wasn't quite Lardon. He dreamed of Lardon's apartment, but it wasn't in the boarding house. He dreamed he felt safe. He dreamed Lardon had told him about a man who was addicted to crack cocaine and that he needed to go and try to help him. He dreamed he took a shower and cleaned the scum off his emaciated body. He dreamed of fresh clothes and a new toothbrush that hurt his bleeding gums. He dreamed of a cheese sandwich and a glass of water. He dreamed that he was more tired than he had ever been. He dreamed he rested his head on an old, worn-out couch.

CHAPTER 50

Ranleigh opened his eyes while still slouched in the car. He grabbed the steering wheel and pulled himself up. Charlotte had gone back to her spot on the curb, patiently waiting for him to wake up. He leaned his head out the open window and called to her.

"Hey," he said, motioning for her to come to the car. Happy to be freed from her boredom, Charlotte stood and ran over. She opened the passenger side door and hopped in.

"Did I leave you there for long?" Ranleigh asked.

"Yes, it was a long time. It's dark. I tried to wake you up, but you wouldn't budge. Jeez, you're a heavy sleeper."

"I'm sorry. Sometimes that happens to me. I just seem to conk out for no reason. A friend of mine thinks it might be a thing called—"

"Narcolepsy," Charlotte interrupted.

"How do you know about narcolepsy?"

"I just do," she told him with an expression that said, don't ask. "I was so bored waiting for you that I started thinking about things again. Mostly about my brother. And I think we need to leave him alone. We should just get out of here, and you can drive me back home. That's what I think. Going in that house might spoil things."

"Do you want to know what I think?"

"Sure," she replied, popping open the glove compartment.

"I think you're right. I don't think you should go into that house. I don't think it's safe. Not only has the place been abandoned forever and would be extremely hazardous for a young girl to walk around in, but we also don't know what kind of shape your brother's in, and no kid should have to see that. I think you should get out of the car and make your way home before it gets too dark."

"But what about you? Aren't you coming with me?" Charlotte said.

"I don't think so. Somebody has to check on your brother. If he's in there, then he's in real trouble. I can't just leave him there. So, I'll let you out here, I'll take a walk up to the house, and check things out. If he's in there, I'll make sure to get him some help. Sound good?"

Looking straight ahead, Ranleigh waited for an answer. When he finally turned back to look at her, she was gone.

The houses gradually thinned out as he continued up the road. Ranleigh checked the address Mr. Lardon had given him: 14 Kramden. He had passed number 10 and then a vast lot that had once been number 12. As it came into view, Ranleigh recognized the house instantly. The framing remained partially intact, but the windows were smashed out, and the roof had completely caved in on the south side.

It was a large house, formerly the most palatial in town before the fire— a fire in which Verna Hewitt had perished. Ranleigh managed to recover a memory of climbing the same stairs now piled in a heap in front of the decaying porch. Back then, he had climbed those stairs to help Verna to his grandmother's car, so they could all make it to the Kinglin Rodeo on time. However, Verna had invited him inside to wait, and he remembered hating being in that house because Verna Hewitt had scared him.

Approaching the rotting woodpile, Ranleigh half expected Verna's corpse to appear slumped in the doorway, beckoning him to retrieve her cane, but Verna Hewitt was long gone.

As he approached the house, Ranleigh regretted not coming better prepared. He wished there had been a flashlight in the car, he would have felt safer. Pushing up with his arms, he managed to hoist himself onto the porch. After getting to his feet and dusting himself off, Ranleigh approached the front door with the gigantic brass knocker.

In addition to the knocker, the door displayed many street signs that had been haphazardly nailed to it. Nine street signs defaced the gigantic red door, some crooked, others upside down. Ranleigh couldn't recall anything about the street signs; they seemed like the handiwork of bored teenagers. Ranleigh turned the handle, using his shoulder to push open the heavy door, and slipped into the front hallway of the Hewitt house. Except this wasn't the Hewitt house at all. It turned out he had stepped into his grandmother's hallway. He called out for her, but there was no response.

Ranleigh walked down the hall toward the kitchen. Glancing from the hall into the living room, he saw that it had been repurposed into a local party room - a place where local teenagers came to have sex and get high. His grandmother's furniture had been replaced by a yellow-stained mattress carelessly tossed in the center of the room, infested with black mould. Two torn-up armchairs exposed the stuffing like innards as if slashed by knives. Graffiti covered the walls, and discarded bottles littered the floor. Turning back toward the kitchen, Ranleigh narrowly avoided stepping on two used condoms lying on the floor in front of him.

As he rounded the hallway into the kitchen, the kitchen which his grandfather had built, a man sitting at the kitchen table startled him. This stranger occupied the table where his grandmother used to lay out her apple pies and butter tarts - the same table where Ranleigh spent many a meal telling her about his life in the city. Now, instead of the day's baking, the table was covered in what appeared to be pieces of handwritten paper, hundreds of them.

"I thought you'd never show up," said the man, his voice sounding as if it had been hand-cranked through a meat shredder.

The figure was undoubtedly a man, but his emaciated form more resembled a creature from the depths of black water. Seated at the table naked from the waist up, tattoos covered his bony arms, and sparse wisps of hair fell to his skeletal shoulders from a balding head. He motioned for Ranleigh to sit.

Ranleigh took his regular seat at the kitchen table and directly across from the man.

"Good of you to come," the man said, extending his hand. "You must be Ranleigh." Ranleigh refused to shake his hand, and the man shrugged, holding up one of the pages.

"I've read a lot about you," he said and laughed out loud.

While briefly taking his eyes off the man, Ranleigh looked around the room. He recognized the drug paraphernalia scattered across his grandmother's stove—discarded needles, burnt square pieces of tinfoil, and brown stained spoons. If Ranleigh had to guess, he would have guessed heroin and he would have guessed wrong. Brad was shooting methamphetamine. Brad caught Ranleigh's gaze and appeared genuinely confused before understanding what Ranleigh was looking at.

"Oh, that," Brad said dismissively. "I guess it didn't take, huh?"

Ranleigh looked at him, perplexed.

"Rehab," Brad clarified.

"Right," Ranleigh said. "Look Brad, your sister is worried about you. Look at you. We need to get you to a hospital," Ranleigh said, looking at the festering black scabs on Brad's forearms.

"No dice, Ranleigh. I'm all done with hospitals."

"I don't think that's a very good idea," Ranleigh replied.

"Ran, Ran, baker's man, hitting the bottom as fast as you can," Brad sang, revealing the stumps of his rotting teeth. "Okay, but before you go, I gotta ask you - dying to, actually - are you out of your fucking mind? I mean, seriously." Brad picked at a festering scab on his arm.

"I found these letters stuffed in the mailbox when I got here. There were piles more tucked behind the screen door. Seems to me like there are hundreds of these things, all written by you. I do want to thank you for some really enlightening reading, man. I mean, when you're as fucked up as I am and stuck in a shithole like this, a place your dealer won't even set foot in, it's always nice to have some reading material to pass the time," Brad said.

Ranleigh didn't know what Brad was talking about, but he recognized the handwriting on the letters as his own - letters he had no memory of writing.

"You're one sorry ass case, Ranleigh," Brad said. "It took me a while to figure it all out. Sometimes it takes me a little longer to figure things out than it used to; I'm not as sharp as I used to be. A little slow on the uptake. Could be the drugs. But these letters seem to state that *we*, by that I mean *you and me*, are not here at all. That I'm not real and that you're not real. These letters, see, appear to be written by one Leigh Meeks, that's you, who thinks this whole thing is one big dream he's concocted. Am I real? Am I not real? Those questions don't matter much to me. I've asked those same questions hundreds of times after the needle goes into what's left of my arm. But the thing that really got my attention, got what juices I have left flowing, is that you, Ranleigh Meeks, are the kid who got me sent up all those years back. You! If it hadn't been for you, I wouldn't be shooting in this shithole."

"That's the drugs talking. I don't know what you're talking about," Ranleigh lied.

"Come on, man. You don't remember that night? You can't sit there and tell me you don't remember the fire. *THE* fire? Where that old bat Verna Hewitt met her maker? You know... *THAT* fire? And how about that accident? There's no fucking way you don't remember the accident. That unfortunate accident. I know you saw it. I saw you. I saw you standing by the swing set when I ran that fucking horse down. But let me tell you something, Ranleigh, the thing I could never figure out—the thing that kept coming back to me over and over and over again while I sat there in prison with those scumbags using my asshole for target practice—was how the fuck did I go down for murdering that cowboy? I never even came close to him. The horse? Sure. Guilty. But was it my fault that the horse took it upon itself to trample that old gasbag to death? My truck was miles away from him. And Verna Hewitt? They should have given me a fucking medal for that one," Brad said.

Ranleigh sat still, his eyes fixed on Brad McGinnis.

"Instead, I end up doing ten years in that cesspool. TEN FUCKING YEARS! And *now* you're here to help me? Fuck you, Jack. But hey, according to these letters, none of that was real. Well, those midnight visits to my cell sure felt real to me. Nocturnal emissions, you might say. And don't get me started on that sister of mine. She left with that bitch, moved to the city, and left me with the old man. Dear old dad—drinking and slapping the shit out of me were his drugs of choice. I wanted to go with her, and she left me here," Brad screamed.

"I didn't have a choice," a voice from the hallway said. Ranleigh spun in his chair to see Charlotte standing behind him. "I couldn't have stayed if I wanted to. Mom and Dad made the decision. If it were up to me, I would never have left you alone with him. Why do you think I've been paying for all those trips to rehab that don't work? Why do you think I still invest my time and my money in a lost cause like you?"

"Why do you think, Ranleigh?" Ranleigh turned back in his chair to see Dallas Cooper, naked from the waist up, deep purple bruise marks blotted across his chest, a bloody bandage wrapped around his head, a needle hanging out of his arm. "So, why does she, Ranleigh?"

Ranleigh suddenly felt like his mind would come apart.

"Coop! Thank God you're here. I don't know what to do with Brad. He needs a hospital, and I don't know how to get him there."

"Why in the fuck would you want to have anything to do with a broken-down cornpone like him, anyway?" Brad McGinnis said from somewhere inside Ranleigh's brain.

"Why does she, Ranleigh?" Coop said.

"Why does she what?"

"Why does she put up with it? Why does she help him?"

"She feels guilty," Ranleigh said.

"Wrong," the cowboy replied.

Ranleigh felt his mind open wide, exposing the circuitry. He didn't want to disappoint his friend by getting this wrong; he was glad to see him and had missed him terribly.

"Answer him, Ranleigh," another voice came from behind him.

Ranleigh turned in his seat, expecting to see Charlotte, but instead, it was his grandmother who stood there.

"What's the answer, Grandma? I don't know the answer." Standing in the doorway with curlers in her wet hair, wearing a pale blue waffle embroidered housecoat, and arms crossed, she replied, "Ranleigh, do you see those letters on the table?"

"Yes, Grandma."

"You wrote them to me from another place. You were having trouble, and you wrote me letter after letter, and I read them all. But because you were in that other place, I couldn't write you back. I couldn't help you at all. Ranleigh, you are in that other place now. Right now, you are sleeping in that other place. You can see all of this, but that's all you can do. Bradley wasn't entirely right when he told you about what he read in those letters—you wrote that this isn't at all real. In a way, it is, and in a way, it isn't."

Another nod was approaching Ranleigh from far away.

His grandmother continued, "The reason we are all here as we are, the reason that we exist, is that you, Ranleigh, didn't have any of these things in your life growing up. There were problems in your home, you didn't have a father or a grandmother or anyone you could turn to. So, when things became intolerable, you made us up. Do you remember when I asked you to go and get Verna on the morning of the rodeo?"

"Yes, Grandma," Ranleigh nodded, barely able to grasp the things she was telling him.

"My dear, when you stepped into that house and she seemed to lose her grip, it frightened you, didn't it? But it was merely the intersection of reality and the dream you had woven for yourself. You see when you dreamt those days in Kinglin, you were actually lying unconscious in a hospital. You had picked up a particularly nasty bout of scarlet fever and you were basically comatose. Verna was the night nurse there, whom you disliked and made a part of your dream, she turned into the puzzled character in her own home. It's understandable, Ranleigh, that you thought she was losing her mind," his grandmother said gently, taking her usual spot across the table from him.

"That morning I made you breakfast, and you appeared to seize up as if you had wandered to a far-off place. You later described it as *losing time*. In reality, all that happened was that you stirred briefly in your hospital bed back home, which momentarily yanked you out of your dream. Are you getting this? So, naturally, years later, the day Jimmy showed you the gun on the bus and Blaireau had docked your pay, the stress caused you to experience this phenomenon again, except this time, it didn't just last for a few days, it started and it never stopped. And oh, how you yearned to be here all the time, and who could blame you, kiddo? You wanted so desperately to be Ranleigh Meeks, the great success. Ranleigh Meeks the fearless. The Ranleigh Meeks you should have been. You sought to escape from your warehouse life, and the larger part of your mind decided this was the best path. But unfortunately, things didn't turn out as you hoped. Things are starting to unravel here, Ranleigh. The real you is in a tough spot, and deep down, you know that. The reason you're seeing me, and Dallas, and Charlotte and Bradley, all together is because Leigh Meeks is on the verge of dying," she said looking directly into Ranleigh's eyes.

"His mind is deteriorating, and so this place, a figment of your imagination, is also starting to crumble. Basic laws no longer hold. You've seen things today that defy basic comprehension, and that, my dear, should tell you that this place is slowly disintegrating."

Ranleigh looked around the kitchen for Cooper, but he was

gone. He was alone again with his grandmother, just the way he had once liked it. He never wanted to leave. Even if what she was telling him was true, he wanted to stay with her forever.

"So, why does she do it, Ranleigh?" she asked again. Ranleigh was fading fast and knew that he would never see her again.

"Because she loves him?"

"Yes, Ranleigh. Because she loves him."

CHAPTER 51

Dream Ranleigh tidied up Brad's mess for the second time that day. All the apparitions had left his grandmother's house. Charlotte, Brad, and Dallas Cooper had all returned to wherever they had come from. He still didn't entirely believe that he wouldn't catch sight of Verna Hewitt hiding around a corner, crouched down, and giggling her mad giggle, but he felt mostly comfortable.

Ranleigh gathered his letters from the kitchen table, lit a fire in the woodstove, and burned them, while his grandmother sliced a piece of apple pie for him and joined him at the table. They didn't speak. Many things still eluded him, but he was happy being with her, even if it was not to last.

Ranleigh scraped the remaining crumbs from his plate, placed it in the sink, and wondered who would clean it in the morning if neither he nor his grandmother were to be there. He no longer cared about the penthouse apartment at the Colonnade, his success, or his money, he knew they were as hollow as his dream. He liked being here and if they could find a way to stay like this forever, that would be just fine with him.

After his grandma returned the last of the pie to the fridge and turned toward him, Ranleigh hugged her one last time. He held on tightly like he did when he was a kid.

Letting go of her, he walked down the hallway to his little bed on the front porch. *No TV tonight, Ranleigh. You don't want to be late for the rodeo tomorrow.* Pulling back the blanket on the narrow cot, he settled himself in. Turning out the light and checking the time on his digital watch, he heard his grandma from the kitchen, "Goodnight, Ranleigh."

Goodbye, Grandma.

That night, Ranleigh dreamt of being surrounded by numerous friends. Lardon had taken him back to the 12 Step meeting, where he felt more receptive than the first time. In his dream, people from diverse backgrounds and walks of life sat around a large table, sharing their stories, their struggles, and their triumphs. He dreamt that when it was his turn to speak, he didn't say much. He apologized for his past behaviour at the meeting, felt he might be ready to learn something, and thanked them all.

After the meeting wrapped up, Ranleigh stayed. He talked with some group members but mostly listened while sipping the watery coffee. He helped clean up by stacking the chairs four high, as instructed by the group secretary at the beginning of the meeting. He managed to congratulate a member who had recently received his one-year medallion after 28 years of trying.

The city had recently banned indoor smoking, so Ranleigh decided to step outside for a quick cigarette before he was missed by Ron. If this was to be Ranleigh's last dream, he hoped it would be a good one. But as it turned out, it wasn't.

CHAPTER 52

The Russian couldn't believe his luck as he occupied his usual spot across the street from the church. From inside his car, he had dialed Leon's number, while patiently waiting for the meeting to come to an end.

The Narcotics Anonymous meetings proved to be easy pickings for a man like Stas. When he first had the idea of selling to addicts looking to kick, he had gone to great lengths, even joining a few groups and faking addiction himself, to sell his drugs to the ideal customer base. It was easy for him to mimic the behaviour of his customers, he had spent many years with them, and his broken English added a certain vulnerability that he could play on. However, he soon realized that the effort required wasn't worth the return. Creating a believable backstory, joining the groups, finding temporary sponsors, and befriending vulnerable addicts teetering on the edge of relapse took too much time and energy.

It was never difficult to find the ones who were looking for any excuse to use. That wasn't the problem, they shared as much when it came time for them to speak. They would lay their hearts bare and tell the room that they had thoughts of using a hundred times a day and that they weren't sure that they could make it another hour without succumbing to the powerful cravings that threatened to overtake them. After the meeting, Stas would be waiting for them. And the best part was that once he completed that first sale, they became customers for life, and they never went back to the meetings to turn him in.

But sitting in those meetings exhausted Stas. After a while, he felt as if he would go out of his mind listening to all the whining and complaining. The never-ending bellyaching got on his nerves.

Fortunately, as luck would have it, Stas arrived late to a meeting one night. He parked his car across the street and decided he just couldn't endure another night in that church basement. He needed a break. While sitting in his car, observing the side door of the church, he noticed a man walking down the street toward him. The man approached the driver's side of Stas's car, and Stas rolled down the window. The man was skinny, unshaven, and wore a baseball cap along with a jacket too thin for the weather.

"Hey buddy, got an extra smoke?" the man asked.

Stas reached into his coat pocket for a cigarette. Although he never smoked himself, he found that having cigarettes on hand helped build trust with the addicts outside the meeting, and he handed them out like candy on Halloween. The transaction was like a dry run. Stas gave the man a cigarette.

"Thanks," the man said, taking the smoke. Stas held a lighter out for him and lit it.

"Very welcome," Stas said.

"Looks like I'm late again," the man continued. "You a member? Friend of Bill's" he asked, gesturing back toward the church with his thumb.

"I am, but I am also late," Stas replied.

"Yeah, probably too late to go in now, right? Wouldn't want to interrupt the speaker or anything," the man said.

"I know exactly what you mean," Stas said. "I'm not sure they're working for me. The meetings."

"You know, I'm glad you said that buddy. If I want to get sober, I can do it anytime I want. And besides, I can't stomach all that Jesus stuff. Bunch of holy rollers in there."

Stas thought to himself, *this guy's a newbie for sure*. He offered the man a ride to wherever he needed to go, but only if he was sure about missing the meeting. The man expressed his certainty, so he hopped into the passenger seat of the warm car, rubbing his hands together in front of the heating vent, and ten minutes later, he was high.

After that first chance encounter, Stas never attended another 12 Step meeting. He would simply wait outside in his car and let them come to him. He had completely underestimated the addict's keen radar for people like him.

Squinting through the tinted glass, Stas was certain it was Leigh. Leigh had exited the meeting after the other group members had thinned out and left. He was lighting a smoke and making his way to the alley beside the church. *Still thinking somebody might see you at a meeting so you're hiding in the alley, huh?* Stas thought.

Everything happened fast. Leigh fell to the ground, face first, smashing his nose into the concrete. The taste of blood filled the back of his throat. His eyes, also soaked in blood, temporarily blinded him. Leigh fought hard to stay conscious and struggled to get back on his feet, but he was losing on both counts.

A hand grabbed him by the hair, pulling him up to his knees. The man (whom he assumed to be a man), ripped the gym bag from his shoulder and held him in place with one hand while doing something with the other. For a brief second Leigh wondered if he was going to be whipped.

Stas spoke, "I teach you to steal from me, yes?"

A small reserve of adrenaline shot up within Leigh, urging him to free himself from the grip. But it was no use. In response to his attempt, he received a hard kick in his lower back, causing his scrotum to retract and his stomach to lurch.

"Try to run again, huh?" Stas wheezed. "Where's money, Leigh? Where's the rest of my product? You little shit."

Stas yanked Leigh's head back, causing his neck to explode in pain. Through the milky blood in his eyes, Leigh saw red stars. Before he had time to answer, or even formulate a good excuse, any excuse, Stas dragged him further down the lane by the hair and out of sight. At the very end of the alley, far from the road and away from the glow of the streetlights, two identical cinder blocks sat about a foot apart, supporting a thin plank of wood. It appeared to be a makeshift workbench or a seat.

"Lie on your stomach, dog," Stas seethed. Leigh obeyed, like a good little doggie. With his free hand, Stas picked up the piece of wood, splintered it over Leigh's head, and chucked it against the side of the church, fully exposing the two cinder blocks.

"Now give Stas your arm," Stas said.

Leigh wasn't so eager to comply with this one. Sit? Sure. Roll over? Absolutely. He might even fetch if it meant staying alive. But putting his own arm over those two blocks? Sorry, Stas, I'll have to take a pass on that one.

"Give me your arm," the Russian yelled. "Give me your arm, and maybe I let you live. Say no, and you die like the dog you are."

Stas hadn't found the gun yet, but he had other ways to kill Leigh. Leigh hadn't yet figured out a way to dispose of the bag and didn't want to leave it at Ron's place, so he was still carrying it around, the gun buried amongst the clothes he stole from Jimmy. Leigh wished that Jimmy had never shown it to him that night on the bus. Leigh lifted his convulsing arm, placed his wrist on the edge of one block and his elbow on the other, and turned his head away. Stas brought his boot down with a crack, and Leigh felt his arm split in two.

The pain exceeded his capacity to comprehend. What he would later remember was the feeling that something was *wrong* inside his body. Not just that his arm was broken or didn't work, but that something was wrong inside. In an attempt to escape this feeling, his body tried to shut him down, but Stas, being somewhat of an expert in pain management back in the old country, delivered a few well-placed blows to keep him awake. Understanding that Stas would do all he could to keep him conscious, Leigh screamed out for the next best thing.

"Pills! For God's sake, Stas! Give me some pills!"

"Stas's pills, fuckface?" Stas laughed, reaching into his sock and pulling out the baggie containing his supply. He dangled them in front of Leigh's face, suddenly snatching them away as he made a grope for them with his good arm. "Tsk, tsk. Not for you, Leigh," Stas laughed again. "You owe Stas. And just for that, I'm taking your other arm too. Then we talk more, yes?" Leigh moaned as Stas dragged him back to the cinder blocks. "Okay, Leigh. Maybe you're right. Have it your way," Stas said, and Leigh could hear him rummaging around in the gym bag.

After finding what he was looking for, Stas yanked Leigh up onto his knees and stood behind him. Leigh's arm dangled beside him in a strange way. He could feel the muzzle of the gun pressed into the back of his skull, and he knew it would all be over soon - the pain, the trap, the anxiety, the endless struggle, the treading water his entire life. Never gracefully, but he had managed, hadn't he?

With his eyes squeezed shut, he recalled what the man with the one-year medallion sobriety medallion had said to him. He told him he needed to let go. Leigh closed his eyes and, for the first time since that morning months ago, silently repeated the OM to himself because he couldn't think of anything else to do.

Leigh heard a sudden, sickening snap. He was still here. Stas lurched forward, and Leigh screamed as he felt Stas roll his full weight onto his severely damaged arm. Leigh's bowels evacuated as he fell forward, re-injuring his nose. More blood.

Rolling away from Stas and onto his good arm, Leigh lost consciousness. But before he did, he turned to look up and saw what he thought was the face of an angel. The face did not belong to an angel. It was Jimmy.

PART SEVEN

ALL THE PRETTY NURSES 1998

CHAPTER 53

January. Toronto General Hospital. Ranleigh Meeks suffered a stroke at some point during or just after the attack, and although doctors were hopeful he would make a full recovery, he remained confined to a wheelchair and experienced difficulty with his speech.

At first glance, his team of doctors attributed the stroke to the brutal blows he had taken during the vicious attack, but further examination painted an even darker picture. Strokes in young adults are rare since they are mostly caused by long-term health problems. The major causes of stroke in individuals in their twenties are traumatic brain injury (which he luckily escaped), drug abuse, diabetes, and generally poor health habits. After conducting a toxicology screen of Leigh's blood, the unanimous verdict pointed to drug abuse.

His arm was another matter. Surgery was held off until the swelling subsided. Fortunately for Leigh, the skin hadn't been broken, but surgery was unavoidable. During the operation, his surgeon repositioned the bone fragments to their original alignment as best he could, then bound them together with metal pins and plates.

Post-operative pain was excruciating, complicated by Leigh's opioid addiction. His medical team relied heavily on non-steroidal anti-inflammatory drugs and local anesthetics, providing a small measure of relief.

Jimmy occupied the oversized, mustard-coloured hospital chair while Leigh sat by the window, a captive of his wheelchair, his gaze fixed beyond the glass. Jimmy brought the only flowers in the room, bright yellow daisies, and set them down beside Leigh on the windowsill.

"So, I hear you might be getting out of here soon. Your doctor said there's a spot for you at an inpatient program for your rehab at St. Mikes on Queen Street. Just a couple of months, they figure," Jimmy said.

Leigh stared out the window.

"That arm looks pretty good now. Man, Stas sure did a number on you," Jimmy said, shifting uncomfortably in the chair.

After a period of uncomfortable silence Jimmy said, "Um, hey, they accepted me into the police force. Turns out Stas had been wanted by the cops for a while, and get this, he had his phone filled with the numbers of all his suppliers, so the cops made a few arrests off that. I think that's why they finally approved my application after it all hit the papers. So, I have you to thank for that, I guess. I got Saeed his job back at the warehouse. After all of this, I figured I might have been wrong about him, and I had a bit of capital with Blaireau, so I thought I'd spend it. That visit from the higher-ups was a real success. Guessed they liked the company name being in all the papers."

Leigh turned his head slightly to look at Jimmy.

"Hey, I'm moving out of my mom's place. Better late than never, right? Late bloomer, that's me. Got a small one-bedroom downtown. Landlord's decent. She read about me after the attack."

Leigh tried to nod, but it was difficult. *Jimmy, you look better,* he thought. *You've lost some weight.*

"Aw, man. I don't know what to say. Can you believe what happened? If I had known this was how things were going to

end up, I would have never introduced you to that maniac,"
Jimmy said.

It's not your fault, Jimmy.

"I mean, what are the odds? That crazy Ron came to the
security office and told me he found you and that you weren't
doing great and that he was going to take you to one of those,
you know, meetings, and that maybe I should meet up with
you guys later for some moral support. I saw you coming out
of the church when I got off the bus. I was going to yell out
when I saw you turn into that laneway, but then I saw Stas
getting out of his car and crossing the street, so I didn't. I
couldn't believe it when I finally got there. He was going to
shoot you, Leigh! I mean, for real. I was really scared. I don't
know what happened. I guess I panicked. I just grabbed the
closest thing I could find and let him have it across the back of
the head. Bam! But your arm, though. I wish I could have been
faster."

He would have killed us both, Jimmy.

"I couldn't run then with all that shit I was eating," Jimmy
said, shifting uncomfortably in the chair. "Well, listen, Leigh, I
gotta go. Need to finish packing. My mom is going crazy with
me moving out and has been trying to guilt me into staying,
but it's time for me to go. Holding on has been tough for me.
She'll get over it, and I'm sure she'll be calling me morning,
noon, and night."

Jimmy stood up and put on his jacket making sure to be
careful with the zipper.

"I'll come visit when they've got you settled in at St. Mikes.
Maybe you'll be out of that chair by then, and we can take a
walk and grab a coffee or something," he said.

Jimmy opened the door to leave and added, "I'll see you
later, Leigh. Give my best to all the pretty nurses."

Leigh watched him go. A silent *thank you, Jimmy. For
everything,* echoed in his heart.

EPILOGUE

Ron pushed Leigh's wheelchair up the church ramp. Ron and another group member named Donny who owned a van made sure to pick Leigh up every Thursday night from the rehabilitation centre and deliver him to the NA meeting. Due to a lack of wheelchair access at the church where his regular meeting was held, Ron decided to switch home groups temporarily to support Leigh. In addition to the meetings, Leigh's doctor had referred him to a psychologist for help with depression and PTSD, who strongly advised against returning to the church where the attack had occurred, another reason for Ron to make the switch.

Because of the rigorous rehabilitation regimen, Leigh felt an improvement in his condition. He looked forward to his release date, as it would mark the second phase of his recovery journey, living in a sober house, where he would learn to live clean and mitigate any potential for relapses. He would continue his stroke management on an outpatient basis. After initial interviews with his drug counsellor, it was decided that Leigh would stay in the facility for a minimum of six months. What lay beyond that period remained uncertain, especially to Leigh. Nonetheless, he had set two goals for himself: to lose the wheelchair and to collect his six-month sobriety chip.

His withdrawal symptoms had significantly subsided since his hospital stay. The doctors had effectively managed his opiate and alcohol withdrawal alongside his stroke symptoms and Leigh had made considerable progress. They had informed him that the detox alone could have been fatal had he not been in the hospital.

Given special permission to leave the rehabilitation centre, Leigh attended the Thursday night meeting, requiring a group member to sign a form as evidence of his attendance. *I'm not sure how far they expect I would get in this wheelchair*, he thought at the time but had kept that to himself. Leigh was learning to listen.

Leigh worked three afternoons a week with a speech therapist and was slowly improving. Although he still experienced difficulties with articulation and word recall, his overall progress was remarkable. The long-term effects of the stroke were expected to be minimal. Physiotherapy posed more challenges, but as Leigh's arm healed, he managed to take a few steps at the center with the assistance of a walker.

Leigh looked forward to Thursday nights. As he embarked on his first year of sobriety, he received ample support and attention from the old-timers, which he sorely needed. While he couldn't contribute much to the setup or tear down of the meeting, he usually managed to stack the books one-handed after the discussion portion of the meeting wrapped up. Ron had agreed to take him on as a sponsee, making himself available twenty-four hours a day. He assured Leigh that they would begin working through the steps together once he settled in the sober house. Ron told Leigh that he wasn't anywhere near out of the woods and needed to get to work on his recovery as soon as he could.

The prospect of making any kind of amends with Blaireau or his landlord made him feel sick to his stomach, but he put his faith in Ron and the process. Leigh still struggled with the God stuff, but Ron told him that if he kept an open mind, his belief in a Higher Power would work itself out in time. Faith in the steps was all he needed to begin.

"Listen, Leigh, your addiction is off in the corner doing push-ups 24/7, just waiting for you to make a mistake and let your guard down," he told Leigh. "The next time, you might not be so lucky." Leigh laughed at that one in spite of himself.

Once inside the church, Ron rolled Leigh to his customary spot at the discussion table before going to grab them both a cup of coffee. A young woman, unfamiliar to Leigh, greeted him as she took the seat beside him. "Hi, haven't seen you before, newcomer?" she asked. Leigh forced a smile and nodded; small talk was still a long way off for Leigh.

"I'm just back myself," she said. "I managed to get myself a one-year medallion a few months back, thought I was cured, and went right back out a week later. Managed to get back in touch with my sponsor and she told me that I probably just needed to do a little more field research, but I'm back now and that's what counts, I guess."

Ron returned with the coffee and set one down in front of Leigh with a straw in it. He gave Leigh a wink and walked over to the door to greet people as they came in. Leigh felt embarrassed by the straw, but the woman paid it no mind.

At precisely 8 PM the meeting began. Ron introduced himself and handed out some sheets for people to read. After the preamble and a reading of the 12 traditions, Ron returned to the sheet in front of him.

"Now, I've asked Tony to read Yesterday, Today and Tomorrow," Ron said.

A middle-aged man with friendly blue eyes took the glasses that were hanging around his neck and put them on. He picked up the laminated sheet from the table in front of him and said, "Hi friends, I'm a grateful addict and my name is Tony."

"Hi Tony," the table responded in unison.

"Hi," he continued. "Okay, Yesterday, Today and Tomorrow:

There are two days in every week about which we should not worry. Two days which should be kept free from fear and apprehension. One of these days is yesterday, with its mistakes and cares, its faults and blunders, its aches and pains. Yesterday has passed forever beyond our control. All the money in the world cannot bring back yesterday. We cannot undo a single act we performed. We cannot erase a single word we said. Yesterday is gone.

The other day we should not worry about is tomorrow. With its possible adversities, its burdens, its large promise and poor performance. Tomorrow is also beyond our immediate control. Tomorrow's sun will rise, either in splendour or behind a mask of clouds, but it will rise. Until it does, we have no stake in tomorrow, for it is as yet unborn.

This just leaves only one day . . . Today. Any person can face the battles of just one day. It is only when you and I add the burdens of those two awful eternities— yesterday and tomorrow — that we break down. It is not the experience of today that drives us mad. It is the remorse or bitterness for something which happened yesterday, and the dread of what tomorrow may bring. Let us therefore live but one day at a time. Thanks."

"Thanks, Tony," the group replied in unison.

Leigh listened as they went around the table. His fellow addicts shared with a level of honesty that was still novel and shocking to Leigh. They shared about their recovery, their fears and their resentments. They shared about the wasted years and the harms done. They gave their personal interpretation of the steps and shared how they managed to stay clean and sober, one day at a time.

As the hour came to a close, everyone had spoken except for Leigh and the woman beside him. Leigh was beginning to feel a sense of belonging, for although the details of each of their stories were different, the story they all told, was his story. He looked over at the sign that hung over the door, *You are no longer alone.* And he wasn't.

"We have a few minutes left if anyone has a burning

desire," Ron said as he readied the collection basket for the 7th tradition collection.

After a moment's silence, the woman beside Leigh put her coffee cup on the table, cleared her throat and spoke.

"Hello everyone. My name is Charlotte, and I am an addict."